THE MYSTERY AND AGENCY OF GOD

THE MYSTERY AND AGENCY OF GOD

DIVINE BEING AND ACTION IN THE WORLD

FRANK G. KIRKPATRICK

Fortress Press
Minneapolis

THE MYSTERY AND AGENCY OF GOD

Divine Being and Action in the World

Copyright © 2014 Fortress Press. All rights reserved. Except for brief quotations in critical articles or reviews, no part of this book may be reproduced in any manner without prior written permission from the publisher. Visit http://www.augsburgfortress.org/copyrights/ or write to Permissions, Augsburg Fortress, Box 1209, Minneapolis, MN 55440.

Cover image © Thinkstock

Cover design: Laurie Ingram

Library of Congress Cataloging-in-Publication Data is available

Print ISBN: 978-1-4514-6573-0

eBook ISBN: 978-1-4514-7977-5

The paper used in this publication meets the minimum requirements of American National Standard for Information Sciences — Permanence of Paper for Printed Library Materials, ANSI Z329.48-1984.

Manufactured in the U.S.A.

This book was produced using PressBooks.com, and PDF rendering was done by PrinceXML.

CONTENTS

Preface		vii
Acknowledgments		xvii
Introduction		1
1.	Otherness and Oneness *Rival Conceptions of God*	23
2.	Establishing the Primordiality of the Agent, Act, and Agency	61
3.	Edward Pols and the Metaphysics of Agency	79
4.	The Metaphysical Conditions for God as Agent	97
5.	How Can God Act in the World? *Divine Action and the Infrastructure of the Socio-Temporal-Material World*	109
6.	Theology and the Discernment of God's Acts in History	129
7.	Coda on the Mystery of God as Agent	151
Bibliography		155
Index		161

Preface

Philip Clayton, contemporary philosopher and theologian of science, claims "theologians have so far paid scant attention to what it means to speak of a divine agent."[1] This does not mean that theologians have not tried to make sense of the notion of divine agency, but the notion of God as an agent who actually acts in the world has had a checkered career. It is a view of God (some would say a rather naïve one) that is clearly implied in the sacred scriptures of the Abrahamic religions: throughout their pages, God is depicted as a personal agent whose actions (ranging from the creation of the universe to its redemption and including many discrete actions in its history) are scattered throughout history and nature. But the notion of God as *someone* who actually acted *in the world* (as distinct from simply having brought the world into being) was subjected to severe criticism with the rise of modern science after the Enlightenment because there was no place in its explanations of happenings in the world for the "intrusions" of a divine supernatural agent in what was otherwise assumed to be a "closed" causal nexus of intramundane happenings. The death of the notion of God as an agent also came about at the hands of many theologians themselves, who could see no future for an idea that not only conflicted with the causal explanations of science but also threatened to obscure the profound and incomprehensible mystery that, for religious purposes, God was assumed to be. By eliminating the notion of God as a "real" agent (except in a metaphorical or poetic sense), theology could avoid being demoted to the level of psychological fantasy. The mystery of God, to which theologians held firm, could (it was almost universally assumed) only be compromised or sullied by making God capable of being understood as an agent in ways that are similar to how we understand ourselves as agents, despite the fact that, again as Clayton reminds us, "only by drawing on the conceptual resources of (human) agency will we be able to conceive what divine agency might be."[2] The fear of an anthropomorphism that would reduce God to the level of the human joined forces with the acceptance of a scientific reductionism that displaced God from the world: the result was to put the notion of God as agent into at least metaphysical limbo, if not purgatory.

1. Philip Clayton, *Adventures in the Spirit: God, World, Divine Action*, ed. Zachary Simpson (Minneapolis: Fortress Press, 2008), 204.
2. Ibid., 206.

For many theologians, what seems to have replaced a metaphysically grounded and robust conception of God as an agent are vague references to the "spiritual" or "transcendent" (sometimes confused with the "transcendental") dimension of life, to a God "beyond or without being," to a numinous religious experience as the non-rational apprehension of the divine mystery lying behind life, and so forth. Without denigrating the non-rational experiential and spiritual dimension of human life, I do not believe it is sufficient by itself to support a notion of God as a personal agent. Any attempt to resuscitate the notion of God as agent is seen by many theologians and philosophers of religion as a crude and unsophisticated return to an outmoded, metaphysically discredited, primitive anthropomorphic view of God that lacks the pizzazz of spiritual mystery and cannot satisfy the religious hunger for contact with something that completely transcends the limits of human thought. Despite the critical condition in which the notion of God as agent now finds itself, I want to return to and defend a metaphysically robust notion of God as agent that, I believe, alone can give specificity to the "spiritual" experience and be consistent with the scriptural witness to God found in the monotheistic religions.

Most theologians simply gave up trying to find a place for God's actions in a world whose explanation has now been entrusted entirely to a scientific reductionist understanding (reducing reality its basic constituent elements, e.g., atoms). In the face of the overwhelming evidence for evolution, for example, theologians have, for the most part, not even dared to suggest the metaphysical possibility of divine action in the world for fear of being called "creationists" or believers in "intelligent design." I will not explore here the metaphysical implications of "creationism" or whether or not God can have a hand in the evolutionary process, but I do believe that theologians need not abandon *every* notion of divine action in the world simply because it can be misused, misapplied, or understood as an interference into the causal order. Almost every attempt to preserve divine action ultimately devolves into some theologically distasteful notion of divine "interference" into or violation of the causal laws that are assumed to be the final and exhaustive explanation of all that takes place in the world. Any attempt to talk coherently of God as an agent whose acts influence the world directly is immediately ruled out of order because it smacks of "creationism" or a fundamentalist reading of the Bible in strictly literal terms. One dare not speak of God acting in the world if one wants to avoid being seen as anti-science or anti-reason.

Almost every writer who has tried to reconcile the methodology of science with belief in God has felt the need to deny that God acts in nature. Quailing under the specter thrown up by anti-theists such as Richard Dawkins that the God who operates as a *super*natural "cause" of events in nature is not scientifically credible, most theologians have tried to find a way around locating divine action *in* the workings of nature, in the unbroken chain of material cause and effect that, allegedly, explains all that happens in nature with nothing left over to be explained in some other way. It is significant that virtually no theologian or philosopher of religion who wants to retain credibility among his peers wants to undermine the universal consensus that God is not to be found as an "intelligent designer" who acts *within* the universe. Credibility might be retained if God is restricted to being the originator or ultimate explanation for the very existence of the universe, but not as a force within the universe once it has begun to exist. Fear of being linked to Creationism and Intelligent Design, associated by most militant anti-theists with a manipulating activist and interventionist deity whom they dismiss as having no explanatory power whatsoever inasmuch as the deity is not a cause alongside other causes, has essentially scared theologians away from any examined analysis of the premises behind the notion that causal law, restricted to finite and measurable causes and effects, is exhaustively explanatory of all that takes place in nature. As John Haught puts it in his *God After Darwin: A Theology of Evolution*, "recent efforts to confront the challenge of evolution by restating or revising arguments for 'intelligent design' are both apologetically ineffective and theologically inconsequential."[3] "The specter of divinity as potentate still hovers over ideas about the 'intelligent designer' whose existence is so tediously debated by creationists and evolutionary materialists."[4]

Nevertheless, Haught does concede that "any coherent faith or theology rightly demands that God be actively involved in the world. . ."[5] For Haught, this demand can be met by theology's provision of "an *ultimate* explanation of why evolutionary creativity occurs in the spontaneous and self-creative manner that it does."[6] He finds this explanation in a process philosophy/theology conception of God as self-emptying, suffering love who makes Godself vulnerable to what God has created as in some sense "autonomously creative." Such an explanation, or theological account of evolution, "in no way interferes with purely scientific explanations" of evolution.[7] If we are allowed to ask why nature is "permitted" to evolve in a spontaneous and self-creative way, theology can provide an answer (the "metaphysics of divine humility"), which is neither

---

3. John Haught, *God After Darwin: A Theology of Evolution* (Boulder, CO: Westview, 2008), 45.
4. Ibid., 48.
5. Ibid., 52.
6. Ibid., 53.
7. Ibid.

materialism nor intelligent design theory, even though Haught insists that it is only in divine humility that "the fullest [divine] effectiveness resides."[8]

I do not intend to follow the details of Haught's explanation, but I do think he is right to want to retain both an explanation of divine action and a refusal to accept intelligent design or creationism as that explanation. Rather than going down the process and panentheistic theology path (which has a lot to recommend it and to which I will give more attention later in the book when discussing the work of Arthur Peacocke and Clayton), I want to go down the path that starts with the notion of the primordiality of action. For in the end, I believe that a robust notion of action is capable of sustaining a real place for scientific explanation of what occurs in the world when action is not taken into account, and of sustaining a notion of divine action that does not entail the dreaded notion of "causal interventionism" from "outside" nature (at least in its typical invocation), a notion that has spooked most of the discussion about how God acts. Only a fully fleshed out notion of action as a primordial category of explanation can preserve a place for divine action *within* and *upon* the world, without becoming an explanation that is a rival to and incompatible with a scientific explanation of worldly events. If human agent-initiated action *per se* is not a metaphysical absurdity, then divine action will not be either. But if the scientific worldview cannot accommodate even free action by conscious human agents alongside of (or, as I will argue, supervening upon and presiding over) causal happenings, then divine action will be thrown out as well. There is, I will argue, a capacious notion of action that includes but goes beyond the notion of merely caused events linked in an unbroken causal chain. Events within that chain will turn out to be best understood as happenings or occurrences in which there is a distinct absence of agent-initiated and agent-superintended actions taking place. Actions, on the other hand, will turn out to be happenings in which agents preside over, supervene upon, and deploy the mechanisms and causal elements of the non-agent dimension of reality in order to carry out their agent-initiated intentions. Their intentions and the acts that fulfill them supervene upon or "comprehend" the causal order without (normally) violating the principles that determine and explain it within its own borders. This is a form of a hierarchical understanding of how agents relate to the causal infrastructure that participates in the field of action presided over by the agent.

Although he uses it for a somewhat different end than I will, Haught argues for the utility of the notion of "hierarchy" in explaining the world. There are some dimensions of reality, he suggests, that are more comprehensive, more

---

8. Ibid., 97.

real, less derivative than others.⁹ The lower levels of reality are "nested" within higher ones. Sometimes known as the "top-down" approach to understanding action, we will see this idea exemplified in such thinkers as Philip Clayton, Arthur Peacocke (who tend toward a panentheistic or process view of God's relation to the world), and in particular in the work of the late philosopher Edward Pols who, while sympathetic to Whiteheadian aims, departs in significant ways from his philosophy. I agree in principle with the top-down or nested approach but find the ultimate explanation of God's relation to the world better explained by the primordiality of the concept of action, not within a process view. Haught employs the concept of "information" to explain how a higher level of reality impacts upon the lower levels, but, however it is done, it "does not interrupt [read 'intervene into'] ordinary physical routines but instead makes use of them in its ordering activity."¹⁰ Peacocke employs a similar concept when he notes that God's interaction with the world is analogous to an "input, a flow of information, rather than of energy."¹¹ The earlier reference to "make use of them" is perfectly consistent with an agent-based view since that is precisely (as Pols will argue) how the hierarchically higher agent carries out the agent's intentions through supervening actions. Actions deploy and utilize the causal infrastructure without either "violating" it or avoiding it entirely by superseding it through some kind of mysterious relation to it. Instead, they use it without being reduced to it.

If the primordiality of agency can be sustained, then we will have found a way around the conflicting assumptions that presently make the evolution/science versus the intelligent design debate virtually unresolvable. Actions that are initiated by "apex beings" acting from the "top down" in order to supervene upon the causal order rather than being causes that intervene into or interrupt the causal order from outside itself will prove to be immune from the anti-theist criticism that God cannot be a supernatural cause violating the causal laws of nature.

If talk of God's relationship with the world is to be retained, many think that it will have to do one of the following:

> 1. Declare God's nature and "actions" as ultimately and incorrigibly mysterious, known not through reason but through the non- or

---

9. Ibid., 69.
10. Ibid., 71.
11. Arthur Peacocke, "God's Interaction with the World," in *Chaos and Complexity: Scientific Perspectives on Divine Action*, ed. Robert John Russell, Nancey Murphy, and Arthur Peacocke (Berkeley, CA: Vatican Observatory and The Center for Theology and the Natural Sciences, 1997), 285.

trans-rational experiences of mysticism. This route leads, at best, to the metaphorical or symbolic use of the terms Agent and Person as applied to God;

2. Try to find a way to "fit" God's action into a world already understood exhaustively by causal law, without challenging the sweep, reductionism, and determinism of causal law explanation by reducing divine action to something that undergirds but does not interfere with the causal structures of the world. This route, I will argue, leads to metaphysical confusion and incoherence and leaves nothing for God to "do" in the world;

3. Develop a robust and metaphysically sound and primordial understanding of God as a real agent whose actions are neither reducible to causal law nor in conflict with it while preserving an appropriate kind of mystery both in God and in our conception of God that will satisfy the religious craving for divine mysteriousness.

It is the third option that I want to explore in this study. Given the confusion produced by reducing complex arguments to sound bites: "religion versus science," "faith versus reason," causal law versus action, or anthropomorphism versus metaphysical mystery, it is impossible in this preface to summarize the results of the exploration I am undertaking without rehearsing in detail the argument itself. Simply, and perhaps misleadingly put, I want to argue that there is a metaphysics of action (reflecting an ontology of being) in which acts are real and distinct from, but not in basic conflict with, causal happenings. Actions do not conflict with causal forces but instead they "utilize" a causal infrastructure, over and through which agents are the primary bearers of action, and from which one can draw out a metaphysically sound notion of God as a primordial agent, who is neither completely ontologically transcendent of the world (metaphysical dualism), nor completely one with it (metaphysical monism).

Every scholar and every practitioner of religion would claim that whatever God is, God is at least mysterious, even the Supreme Mystery opaque at some deep level to rational comprehension. The mystery of God is an article of faith in virtually all religions. At the same time, however, for religious people the divine mystery is almost always attenuated or qualified by an equally important article of faith and that is that God can be known, at least to some extent, especially if God chooses to make the divine self known. If God were totally, absolutely, and exhaustively mysterious, then no concept of God could be developed, no relationship with God would be possible, and God would, for all practical purposes, be useless to the living of our lives. (To say that God is *absolutely* mysterious is to say nothing about God, since a totally mysterious "something" is just that, totally mysterious. And about that which is totally mysterious nothing can be said because there would be no way to judge what is said as true, or false, or even meaningful.) In the theistic religions, God's mystery is always tempered or qualified to some degree by the actual worship practice of religious believers who pray to God; thank God; offer their lives to God, affirm creedal convictions about God, and are inspired by stories in their scripture that depict God as somehow deeply implicated in their lives and in the history and nature of the world. One both thanks God for what God has done, is doing, and is believed will do in the future while at the same time acknowledging that God is not *completely* subject to rational understanding. God is not a *product* of human thought and can, if God chooses, remain beyond total and exhaustive rational comprehension. But divine choice implies divine agency, which in turn presupposes that God's very mystery is inherent in the primordiality of God's being an agent. The mystery and the affirmation of God as agent go hand-in-hand in the actual lives of most theistic believers. The challenge is to make sense of both without eliminating one at the expense of the other.

There is something religiously right and appropriate about claiming some kind of mystery in the divine. The trick is to locate that mystery in the right place. I want to explore how the mystery of God is located in, preserved, and qualified by three distinct views of God. I will argue why one of them is more persuasive than the others in retaining both the divine mystery and the possibility of a personal agent-to-agent relationship with God. I will focus my exploration on the primordial or basic concept of agency: the capacity of any agent, including God, to act in and upon the world and upon the human agents whom God's action empowers and fulfills. Out of God's agency will emerge what, in my opinion, is the appropriate kind and location of religiously significant mystery.

Given the importance of having a developed and coherent understanding of God, I intend to establish the metaphysical power and primordiality as well as the religious significance of a view of God as a personal agent. In doing so, I will argue that this view retains a meaningful degree of the mystery required of a religiously acceptable concept of God. In order to make my case, I will show how the concept of God as personal agent meets the challenge posed by two more prominent and classically established views of God: the dualist and the monist.

There are, I believe, three logically distinct basic or metaphysical views of God: first, the dualist view of God as radically and wholly "Other," as ontologically transcendent of everything other than Godself, a God beyond or without Being; second, the monist view of God as undifferentiated oneness, One without a second; and, third, the pluralist or agent view of God as the primordial and supreme personal agent existing as creator and sustainer of but also as *standing alongside* (in a sense to be defined further) other beings and agents within a common ontological space, a commonality of a field of agency that is required for relationality between personal agents. While not in itself an argument in defense of the notion of God as personal agent, I believe it is relevant that this is the view of God implicit in the monotheistic Abrahamic traditions. While the dualist and monist views quickly entice the mind into the apophatic mystery (the mystery beyond words) of God as beyond all human comprehension, the agent view appears on first glance as hopelessly anthropomorphic, naïve, and primitive. I intend to make the case, however, for the metaphysical power of this agent view of the divine even in the face of its more established and more intellectually sophisticated competitors and detractors.

I will do so primarily by mining the work of three much neglected contemporary philosophers of action or agency: Raymond Tallis, Edward Pols, and John Macmurray.[12] I will also explore, though somewhat less copiously, the work of process-oriented panentheists Arthur Peacocke and Philip Clayton who also develop a concept of divine agency on a somewhat different model. Through a creative synthesis of their work, I will show that the primary and basic sense of power in reality is the power of agency (not causality, which is a subset of agency), a power that can only be exercised by an agent.

Developing these three philosophers' conceptions of the agent, the act, and agency, I will then challenge the overriding and dominant assumption that casts its shadow over all talk of God's actions in the world. That assumption, which I will argue is ultimately unjustified, is that God's actions in the world must "fit into" the causal structure of the world, that a "causal joint" must be found for God's action in the world in order to avoid what is usually taken to be unacceptable divine "interference," "intrusion," or "intervention" into the causal structures of the world. This assumption presumes the ontological or primordial primacy of causality to which action must conform or fit into. This is such a pervasive assumption that it will take a kind of philosophical shock treatment to think differently about action in relation to causality. I will therefore offer an initially audacious and radically different understanding of

---

12. These three thinkers, from all that I can tell, do not reference each other (Macmurray died in 1976 and Pols in 2005) so my integration of their work has not and might not ever have received the approbation of any of them.

action drawn primarily from Pols's notion of action as an agent's *deployment* of the causal infrastructure over which the agent presides and through which the agent exercises supervening power, attempting to realize certain intentions through actions that pervade and utilize that infrastructure. When the agent acts, from a position at the apex of the causal structures, the agent's act both pervades and unifies the elements of that causal infrastructure, bending them toward the enactment or realization of the agent's purpose. In this view, acts don't *fit into* a pre-existing causal order: instead they *preside over, supervene upon*, and *utilize* the causal order *through which* they transmit the intention of the agent who originates them and through which they *express*, realize, or manifest, his or her intentions. This notion of action allows us to set aside the plethora of attempts that have dominated most of the contemporary discussion of divine action and that have been constrained to try to fit God's action into a pre-existing causal structure that, ever since Kant, has been seen as opaque and closed to free action, both divine and human. To my knowledge, contemporary philosophers trying to find a way to fit God's action into the world have almost completely overlooked or vastly underappreciated this argument. By failing to treat the power of this argument seriously, they are left with basically unsatisfactory notions of divine action as "interfering with" or "intervening in" the causal order, thus leaving divine action a fundamental mystery (ironically without noticing that this also leaves human action a fundamental mystery). This, I will argue, is not the mystery of God that is religiously compelling. I will argue that the mystery of God should be found elsewhere: not in *whether* God can act or whether God's acts are subject to metaphysical comprehension, but rather in *why* God in the depths of God's personhood and freedom *chooses* to act, and to act as God does, and what our responses to God's actions ought to be.[13]

I will conclude by showing how the notion of a divine personal agent retains all the mystery necessary for a worshipful and religious significant response to that reality we call God because we believe we have been encountered and challenged by divine actions that call us into relationship with their author. This is the deepest and most religiously significant mystery of all:

---

13. I have tried to avoid using any gendered pronouns for God. While I believe that God is a personal agent, this belief does not, in my opinion, commit me to affirming that God has a specific gender. To avoid the problem of gendered pronouns, I have chosen to use "Godself" for God even if the price for doing so is, given centuries-long tradition of using the masculine pronoun for God, a small bit of syntactic awkwardness. I have not, of course, changed the gendered pronouns for God in the works by other authors that I cite from time to time.

the mystery of personal relationships and their most important and mysterious characteristic—love.

Acknowledgments

I would like to acknowledge the encouragement for this project by Professor William Power and Dr. Lee Wallace, who reviewed original drafts of the manuscript. Special thanks are owed with great gratitude to Professor Edmond LaB. Cherbonnier, for starting me off in the right direction of thinking about God as Agent nearly fifty years ago. I am also especially indebted to the scholarly work of Edward Pols and William Alston on the notions of agency and action. Finally, I would like to acknowledge the wise advice of Mike Gibson of Fortress Press in helping to shape my original proposal into an acceptable manuscript and his editorial colleagues Lisa Gruenisen and Marissa Wold for getting the manuscript into shape for publication.

Introduction

Explorations of Divine Agency and Divine Mystery

One of the most problematic dimensions of religious belief is the conviction that God is so utterly mysterious that God cannot be comprehended by the human mind and, at the same time, is so utterly personal that our lives are incomplete without the deepest kind of relationship with God. Religious belief is often caught between the allure of the mystery of God and our desire for a personal relationship with God. And yet, there is no more serious disconnect at the heart of monotheistic theologies than the deeply personal religious practice of praying to God as *Someone* who has, can, and will *do* things or *act* in some way in response to prayer, and a theological conviction that the divine mystery is so deep and so beyond our ability to comprehend that God cannot be the kind of reality who can *literally do* anything at all because "doing" (acting) is not possible for the kind of reality that God, in God's deepest and most cognitively inaccessible being, essentially *is*. The fundamental mystery of God toward which most religious people are drawn, as a moth to a flame cannot, it is believed, be resolved by reducing God to the status of an agent who acts in the world. Without being quintessentially mysterious, God would become simply one item in our world subject to our conceptual and practical manipulation. In some very profound way God, many insist, *must* be beyond our conceptual reach while remaining religiously connected to us in some way. The fullness of God cannot be caught by our conceptual webs, but God must remain in some deep relationship with us if God is to have any relevance to our deepest religious aspirations and desires. How to articulate these twin commitments has been the problematic heart of the western monotheistic theological tradition.

Religious practitioners seem to want two things simultaneously that are extremely difficult to hold together conceptually: they want a God to whom they can relate and they want a God who utterly transcends the limitations of the ontological conditions in which they as human beings exist, including the limitations of their language, conceptions, and knowledge. I want to acknowledge both of these yearnings by showing how they are reflected in three apparently disparate views of God (though two of these views, I shall argue, constantly intertwine, play off against each other, and eventually collapse into one, even though both have been treated historically as superior to the third view [of God as "literally" a personal agent] which is usually dismissed as far too unsophisticated to be taken seriously). I will not argue that only one of the three (or two) is the right one, but I do want to show that the stepsister view of God as personal agent has a previously underappreciated metaphysical power that, when appropriately exploited and deployed, makes it a strong contender for philosophical/metaphysical appeal. At the same time I believe it more successfully captures the practice within monotheistic traditions of praying and relating to God as a Someone whose literal acts make a decisive difference to them and to the world. The challenge to this third view is how it can retain the necessary aura of mystery and incomprehension that seem to the adherents of the first two views of God to be absolutely essential if their views of God are to be taken seriously.

My argument, in a nutshell, will be that by drawing on the ontological or metaphysical[1] *primordiality* (the basicality) of *personal agency*, one can derive a concept of God that does justice both to God's relationality through action and to God's profoundest mystery. I will also argue that a persistent misunderstanding of agency has hamstrung attempts to "fit" God's action into the causal nexus of worldly events, to find what some scholars have called the "causal joint" between divine action and the cause-and-effect matrix within which natural events are located and understood. I will show that there is a different, and heretofore, radically underappreciated understanding of action that does away with the problems that attempting to fit divine action to a causal joint have caused.

I have used the word "metaphysical" to refer to the notion of personal agency here, simply to denote a view of the structure and nature of reality as a whole. It will be crucial to this exploration of God's nature as agent to remember that there is more than one respectable metaphysical view. Everyone operates, whether at the virtually unconscious level or at the level of the highest philosophical speculation, with some kind of metaphysical view.[2] For example, one metaphysical view is that reality is nothing but bits of matter and all explanation of reality is materialistic. Another is a more dualistic view that reality consists of matter plus conscious beings whose consciousness is not

---

1. I use the words "ontological" and "metaphysical" because they connote the fundamental "stuff" of reality: what is really real and how it is conceived by the human mind. They are used by philosophers and rather than invent a new set of terms, I intend to stick with these though I will try to make sense of them in a way that sometimes eludes the best efforts of philosophers to make their terminology "user friendly." Whatever reality turns out to be, God must be implicated in, under, through, or with it (though exactly how is the heart of the debate).

2. In a later chapter, I will discuss how some contemporary theologians, such as Wolfhart Pannenberg, deal with the issue of metaphysics and theological claims.

reducible to matter. Metaphysical views disagree about whether freedom to act is real or an illusion. Each of these views entails a whole host of metaphysical assumptions and principles. If a religious person expects her relation to God, to other persons, to the world, and to her religious tradition or community to have something to do with what is true and real, she will have (or hope to have) a metaphysical view, even if it remains implicit and not yet fully developed. I will assume that the metaphysical view of reality that is most congenial to the monotheistic traditions of Judaism, Christianity, and Islam is one that entails or depends upon a notion of God *as* a personal agent, and not just in a metaphorical but in a literal, direct, and primordial sense.

I will argue that metaphysical dualism, and its principle of ontological transcendence, ultimately misrepresents and distorts the implicit metaphysical view (it is rarely brought to the level of explicit awareness and articulation) in the liturgical and scriptural texts that God is one agent among other agents and is appropriately understood by a literal application to God of the concepts of agency and agent. (The term *literal* will need some unpacking, but the thrust of my argument is that the differences between the divine agent and human agents are real and religiously significant but are not so categorical as to undercut the common application of the concept of "agent" to both God and human beings.)

But this argument goes very much against the grain of western theology and will be very difficult to establish because it seems at best counterintuitive and, at worst, a falling back into primitive superstition (especially an anthropomorphism dreaded by nearly all serious theologians and philosophers), which not only fails the test of metaphysical sophistication, but can't even take the test in the first place because it isn't adequately equipped with the right concepts. In addition, it will be taken as denying or avoiding a recognition of the mystery of God, a mystery without which, it is claimed, God would not be worthy of worship and not worth the trouble of thinking about. The argument for the primordiality of personal agency applicable to both human agents and the Divine Agent is, nonetheless, essential if we are to bring credibility and religious utility to our understanding of the divine with whom we want to enter into the closest possible relationship without losing any of the mystery that has attracted religious believers to the concept of God from the beginning, although the nature of that mystery will necessarily have to be redefined and relocated. God must satisfy our craving for contact with the most basic reality and our conviction that God lies, in some crucial ways, outside our cognitive grasp and manipulation. How to satisfy both inclinations is the task of philosophical theology. If we cared nothing about a relationship with God, the problem would be solved simply by finding ways of articulating the divine mystery (despite the internal contradiction in trying to do so), but the essence of relationality is the co-presence of at least two beings, neither one annulling nor being reduced to the other. But how can God be God, in the traditional view, if God is in a relationship with (without being limited by) that which is ontologically and totally other than Godself?

For those who want to stress the mystery of God, it is not helpful to say that God is the kind of "being" who does not act because even to think of God as "a" being (or entity) is, for some philosophers of religion, a profound mistake. God, for them, is not "a" being but instead is the ground of being, or act-of-being, Being-Itself, or even "that" which is beyond being, other-than-being. God is the Wholly Other and so other that God cannot even be compared with that which God is other than. Therefore, many would argue that to even to think of God as one who does things—as an agent—is a fundamental confusion of conceptual categories. It confuses God with all that constitutes the "reality" that God transcends. It makes God an entity, a subject/object[3] *within* the ontological conditions that apply only to non-divine subjects/objects, thus reducing God to their ontological level and trapping God within the metaphysical conceptual categories appropriate to them but not to God.

This approach to the mystery of God seems to have everything going for it. It appeals to a deep intuition in all serious religious thinkers that God can at best be "glimpsed" or "intuited" but never comprehended through our metaphysical lenses. There is something about a mystery that always remains just outside the reach of concepts and explicit consciousness. There is something about quotidian thinking that suggests (even demands) a reality beyond conceptual reach, a limit to thinking, a horizon of thinking or being, a depth, transcendence, and otherness that cannot be grasped *within* the limits of human thought. Any metaphysical view that brings God within the reach of human thought and direct experience (as one being in relation to another) is degrading, unsophisticated, simplistic, naïve, and primitive, unworthy of serious metaphysical consideration. I want to recognize the strength of this approach to the mystery of God but ultimately to question whether it is adequate to our experience of God as one standing in relation to us and whether it is metaphysically coherent.

The disconnect or tension between trying to relate to God as a personal agent and thinking of God as beyond personal agency has long been part of

---

3. I say subject/object because in one sense all personal entities are subjects to themselves and yet objects to others. As a personal self I am a subject with subjective qualities – emotions, thoughts, intentions, etc. that are uniquely mine and at the same time I am an object for other subjects who may or may not discern these subjective qualities correctly or 'objectively'.

my own personal religious life and theological convictions. But I have grown increasingly dissatisfied with this disconnect at both personal and conceptual levels. I have come to suspect that the disconnect is based on a fundamentally flawed concept of what God "must be" to be God, a flaw that I believe can be remedied by utilizing a different basic or primordial conceptual category, that of personal agent, for understanding God.

I want to explore the reasons for this disconnect with an eye toward resolving it by invoking what I will call the *primordiality* of personal agency, both as fact and as concept. By primordiality I mean simply that personal agents[4] are a non-reducible, basic, ontologically fundamental, elemental fact of life and that the concept that reflects that fact is itself non-reducible, incapable of either being broken down into more basic "parts" or gone beyond by a more transcendent concept intended to represent that fundamental fact. A primordial category is one that doesn't need to be explained from beyond itself by something more basic or elemental or more transcendent and exalted.

My argument will be that the concept of God as personal agent is primordial and sufficient for representing God. It is not derived from or constructed out of more basic elements. It is a basic and fundamental concept that represents a basic and fundamental fact about God that cannot be supplemented or completed by categories drawn from elsewhere. Personal agency is the "north pole of human thought": you can't go beyond it to a more essential or inclusive category for thinking about reality. And, as I will argue, the very fact that thinking about these matters must itself begin in and presuppose the personal agency of the thinker is a clue to the basicality of agency in structuring our reflection about ourselves, other agents, and the world in which we exist. Doing, it turns out, must be more basic than thinking since thinking is itself an act or a doing, while doing is not always an act of thinking (though it is usually preceded or guided by thinking). Acting is therefore inclusive of thinking while thinking is exclusive of doing (except in the sense that it is itself a doing). If we follow through on the full implications of this fact, we will eventually arrive, I will argue, at the notion that God's fullness and mystery is best reflected in the notion of God as primordially a personal agent. It will follow that the mystery of God is essentially the mystery of any

---

4. I will use the terms "agent" and "personal agent" interchangeably except where some distinctions will need to be drawn for clarity in particular contexts. To be an agent, I will argue, an entity must have consciousness and intentionality (i.e., purposiveness). Only persons have both. Many beings, of course, bring about effects by their movements in relation to other beings. A molecule affects and effects changes in the organic world in which it moves. But we should not call a molecule an agent since presumably it does not bring about these effects consciously and purposely.

personal agent whose freedom to intend new courses of action always keeps God one step ahead of scientific predictions and reductions. And the mystery of God as agent is deepened precisely by the universal scope of God's power and knowledge. Whether it is as robust a mystery as some theologians would like is another question.

Appropriate Anthropomorphism

However, there is another equally significant and powerful inclination in religious life. It is a strongly felt, almost irresistible inclination not to settle for a notion of God that seems, on the surface, so superficial, simple, limited, particular, and finite as the notion of God as a personal agent. It seems too confined by the structures of the finite, spatio-temporal material world (what I will refer to from here on out as the STMW) in which we exist and have our being. It is, frankly, too *anthropomorphic* to serve the deepest inclinations of religious feeling: too laden by the application to God of attributes that derive from limited, finite, contingent *human* personal agents. As human persons, we are enmeshed in and limited by the finite world of spatial-temporal-material conditions. We are also, in the theologies of the monotheistic religions, too sinful to be the basis for concepts about a God who transcends all human limitations and failings.

According to most philosophers of religion, anthropomorphism is probably the single most significant failing in any argument for God as a personal agent. It fails the test of theological/metaphysical sophistication precisely because it derives a concept of God from our experiences of ourselves as personal agents "trapped" in the STMW. And yet thinking anthropomorphically is virtually inescapable if we find in the world beings that share with us basic personal characteristics. Let's assume for the sake of argument that the basic attributes of human personal agents are consciousness, will, and purposiveness or intentionality (i.e. the ability to intend courses of action and to carry them out). If we assume that anthropomorphism is the application to some being(s) other than ourselves of characteristics that fundamentally define us as human beings (personal agents), then clearly anthropomorphic qualities are inappropriate when applied to rocks or trees.(I exclude for the sake of argument the claim by some Buddhists that trees and plants are sentient beings.) Virtually everyone agrees on that point. These objects *lack* something that human personal agents have. So then the question becomes, what is it about consciousness, will, and the ability to intend (and effect) courses of action that is inappropriately applied to God? Does God *lack* these attributes? Most theists would deny that God lacks them. But they are uncomfortable saying that God *has* them in the same way we have them. Now, as we shall see, there are two views of God (the dualist and the monist, which eventually collapse into each other) that ultimately do conclude that God lacks these attributes because, they will argue, God is not the *kind* of reality who has attributes appropriate in the STMW since having these kind of attributes is itself a limitation and a deficiency. Lacking a limitation is no slur on God. But to hold to the monist or dualist view is to deny to God any attributes that constitute the personal agent in communion with other personal agents. This, I would suggest, is far too high a price to pay to maintain the mystery of and difference between God and what is other-than-God.

But if we do not go all the way toward extreme dualism or monism, we are left with a view of God as a being who has attributes and then the question becomes *which attributes* are appropriate for a divine being. And at this point, anthropomorphism becomes inescapable. Either God has consciousness, intentionality, love, and so on, or God does not. Either God is compassionate or God is not. Now the *degree* or *extent* of God's consciousness or compassion may be radically (though not ontologically) different from that of human consciousness and compassion. God's love may so far exceed our ability to love that it is metaphorically appropriate to say that God's love should not be compared to human love. But there must be some commonality between God's love and ours if our understanding of divine love is to have any meaning at all, and this commonality is the basis of an *appropriate anthropomorphism*. After all, what positive meaning does "greater than personal" have? What is *greater* than the personal (intentionality, consciousness, will, love, etc.)? Unless one can specify the content of something "greater" than these things, one is committed, whether one likes it or not, to some kind of anthropomorphism. The question will not be *whether* anthropomorphism is appropriate, but what kind of anthropomorphism is.

It is significant, I think, that even those scientific reductionist attempts to explain human behavior as mechanistically or biologically determined use anthropomorphic language (perhaps inadvertently) even while denying the reality of essential personal attributes to human persons. Genes, for example, are said to "intend" their own survival and reproduction. The only way to avoid anthropomorphic language is to think of something other than ourselves as having no personal agent attributes at all. And in many instances this denial of personal characteristics is absolutely appropriate. Rocks, for instance, cannot be said to intend, plan, think, reflect, desire, regret, or hope, and thus anthropomorphic terms do not apply to them. Conversely, the only way to avoid anthropomorphic language for God is to assume that God has no personal characteristics at all: God does not intend, plan, think, reflect, care, or love, and so on. But no theistic view of God has denied *all* of these characteristics to God, though they often have to be stretched beyond their "normal" usage. The question is whether this "stretch" carries them so far beyond their fundamental meaning as to render them literally meaningless.

So the issue is not anthropomorphism as such but the degree and kind of anthropomorphism that is appropriate to subject/object to which it is applied. When is it metaphysically appropriate to characterize God as personal, conscious, loving, intending, acting? A lazy or simplistic anthropomorphism is to be avoided but the attempt to transcend anthropomorphism entirely is impossible and misguided. A sophisticated and carefully worked out anthropomorphism will, I believe, yield a view of God that is both metaphysically and religiously satisfying. But the proof is in the pudding as they say.

There is a drive in all religious people to reach beyond this finite world of enmeshment and entanglement toward a reality that utterly transcends it, striving toward a horizon, an absolute otherness from us, that in some sense stands above, beyond, or under all that constitutes the finite world, and which is itself not *part of* that world as one entity alongside other entities, and therefore not reflected adequately in any conceptual categories originating in and conditioned by that world. Some part of my spiritual being wants a union with God that is *more than* a relationship *between* God and me (since a relation of betweeness presupposes God as an "other" [i.e., as not-me] yet existing within the same general ontological space as me, even though radically different from me in certain basic ways). Relationality always necessarily limits the beings that are in relation since, to be in relation, each must have some degree of ontological independence (or, as we say colloquially, having one's own "space") in relation to the others. Instead, what some religious people reach for is a union with that initially appears as "other" but in which I may eventually become fully absorbed *into* God, a union in which the distinction between myself and God is overcome and I become one, literally, *with* God in whom my being participates in a undifferentiated way. I, in effect, lose my ontological independence as an independent, individualized self and am absorbed into God without remainder. I want to acknowledge God's initial and apparent otherness and then cross the gap that divides us by becoming one with God, not a being *in* relationship to God. This is where, I will argue, *ontological dualism* (the radical otherness of God to the world) eventually collapses into *ontological monism* (the undifferentiated oneness of God, which includes and even extinguishes the otherness of what initially seemed to be separate from God).

While ontological dualism seems initially the polar opposite of ontological monism, they are, I will argue, fraternal twins, crossing and recrossing each other, fusing and separating, merging and distinguishing one from the other as each tries to do justice to the absolute otherness of God (as seen from the human point of view) and the oneness of God (as seen from the divine point of view). It will be virtually impossible to treat one without implicitly also treating the other since they are so metaphysically close despite their initial appearance of difference.

If, as I will argue, the notion of agency is a primordial or basic notion, then to achieve *immersion in* God (not a relationship "with" God that continues to presuppose a distinction *between* me and God), then we have to push beyond agency to get to the core of what it means to be God. But the more we move outside or beyond the category of agency, the more we replace the primordiality of that concept with something else. And that something else is articulated best by the mystics and some philosophers who want to take thought to its very roots in a reality that encompasses it, saturates it, or is presupposed as the unarticulatable horizon or ground for it. And that reality is a single undifferentiated oneness in which even the initial divine otherness is ultimately swallowed up.

I want to draw out, in effect, an important claim regarding the difference between monism and dualism made by Mark C. Taylor who said,

> The foundational principle of immanence entails a monistic schema in which God, self, and world are different manifestations or expressions of the same underlying reality. Transcendence [what I've called radical Otherness] shatters monism by introducing a radical Other, which forms the foundation of the principle of oppositional difference constitutive of every dualism. The monistic and dualistic schemata illuminate . . . the contrasting ways in which God or the divine seems to disappear. In monism, God and the gods disappear by becoming indistinguishable from the world—when everything is sacred nothing is sacred. In dualism, God and the gods vanish by becoming so distant that they are inconsequential and thus disposable—when the divine is totally absent, nothing is sacred.[5]

---

5. Mark C. Taylor, *After God* (Chicago: University of Chicago Press, 2007), 133.

While apparently quite different on the surface, the assertion of God's radical otherness will, I argue, collapse into an undifferentiated oneness that is both God and everything that appears (initially but misleadingly) as other than God. Otherness and identity are fraternal twins whose existence is mutually implicated even though on the surface they seem to be bitter rivals.

It is when the undifferentiated oneness that many mystics extol becomes *identified* with God that we run into difficulty in preserving the notion of God as agent. An agent God cannot *be* being-itself, but we'll see many reasons why many people have thought this to be the case. In order to preserve God's radical otherness, they opt for discarding the notion of divine agency or retaining it only as a metaphor whereas I will opt for treating the notion of God as absolutely other or, in its collapse into being-itself, as a derivative metaphor, not a primordial concept. I am willing to refer to God, who is non-metaphorically a personal agent, for heuristic and meditational reasons, by the symbol of God as being-itself.

An important clarification will need to be made between thinking God as supernatural, outside, above, or beyond the world and thinking God as the ground of being in whom all beings participate or subsist. In the first option, God is, in some sense, still "a" being since God is not identical with any or all of the finite beings who are limited in a vast number of ways (e.g., with respect to duration, power, knowledge, etc.). As long as those finite beings have a real existence, God must be differentiated from them. In the second option, God is not "a" being at all but is postulated as the ground or horizon of being who, without existing as "a" being, makes possible the existence of individual beings and the "world" in which existing beings "are." (This making possible is not necessarily "causing" other beings to exist because the notion of being a "cause" is conceptually problematic for God if God is conceived as beyond the distinction of cause and effect or beyond the distinction between transcendence and the other, which God transcends.) The difference between the God who is different by virtue of being a transcendent being and the God who is different by virtue of being the ground of being from whom other beings are not distinguished by differences of natural versus supernatural is at the heart of much of the difficulty in formulating a notion of God that is other than that of God as personal agent.

The Experience and Concept of God

I believe both the inclination to think of God as a personal agent and one to think that God must surely be more than that exists in many religious believers, myself among them. And so I write in the first person about all this, drawing both upon my religious experience and my forty years as a philosophical theologian who has wrestled intellectually with these issues. I am writing this book because of the seriousness with which I have taken the *concept* of God (and I believe also the *experience* of God) in my own life and thinking. I have struggled at both a personal and a theological level about how to reconcile the disconnect between the common assumption that God cannot act in the world as we normally understand action, and the religious practice of assuming that God has acted (and continues to do so) in the lives of religious people and their communities. I want to share my own struggle with this disconnect and the theological/philosophical resources that have helped me in that struggle. And in the process I want to point to some ways in which I think the worst effects of the disconnect might be mitigated, if not dissipated. I will press especially strongly on a different way of conceiving action that does not produce the traditional misunderstandings about "fitting" action (divine or human) into a closed causal structure. That different way, outlined in its basic form by the late philosopher Edward Pols, sees action as the utilization of (not a subordinate element in) the causal infrastructure. As such, action is not fit *into* causality, but causality is fit into the overarching intentionality of the agent whose acts exploit, utilize, and deploy causality. A complementary, but not identical, understanding is developed by a panentheist approach advocated by Arthur Peacocke and Philip Clayton and will be given some attention later on.

I want to think simultaneously of God as a personal being with whom I can have a deep, transformative, and fulfilling relationship and as having or being "more" than anything I can possibly conceive "within" the world I inhabit because I know the limitations of the human mind and of the other finite objects with which I have daily interactions. I don't want to encapsulate God in humanly derived concepts of thought because I want to do justice to the mystery of God, but I also don't want God to become so remote or "other" by means of a conceptual virtuosity that both affirms and annuls the power of thought to think of God that I can no longer have a personal relationship with God. Similarly, I don't want to encapsulate any personal agents in forms of thought that deny them the freedom and power to escape from restricted understandings that have derived from reductionist categories of thought that have no place for personal mystery or freedom of action.

Religiously, I listen to and recite the words of the creed and believe them when they affirm God as the one who created the world, not as an extension of Godself but as a reality over against God (i.e., ontologically other than or distinct from God) though radically dependent upon God's willingness to sustain its existence from moment to moment.

I have found after forty years of teaching and research that most academic writing strives to attain an objectivity in thought at the expense (or at least a hiding) of the fact that any reflection on God is self-involving and thus that the experience of the self (myself in this case) cannot be set aside. This does not mean that one reflects on the experiences one has without the aid of highly polished intellectual skills, methods, and concepts. They are essential to one's very being as a philosopher or theologian. But writing drily and abstractly about one's engagement with God (or at least with the concept of God; the distinction is one that will need much greater elaboration) has become, for me, a dead end and no longer worth the effort if done in isolation from the *practice* of religious living. At the heart of the religious life (at least in the theistic religions) is prayer to God and a sense that one is responding to the actions of God as revealed in the self-involving recital of God's actions in the past, as these are represented in a written text taken by the religious community to be some kind of holy scripture (such as Tanakh, the New Testament, the Koran, and other monotheistic religions such as Zoroastrianism, Sikhism, and even some forms of Hinduism, to name a few).

Prayer and thanksgiving (as distinct from meditation) presume that there is Someone there to whom the prayer or thanksgiving is addressed and that the addressee will (or at least has the capacity to) respond to the prayer by *doing something*. (What is done may not, of course, be exactly what the petitioner has asked for.) Creedal affirmations are presumed to be "about" Someone whose actions (e.g., creation, liberation, covenant, reconciliation, healing, comfort, salvation) are affirmed as being of ultimate significance to the believer and the world as a whole. Many forms of meditation, on the other hand, do not presuppose the existence of some *other being* with whom the meditator is in relation or about whom the meditator is thinking.

And yet, most theological reflections on God have assumed that to *be* God in the first place, the Someone who is God cannot "do" things, cannot act in the world, in anything like the way human agents do things and act in that same world. The world that is supposedly open to human action is closed to divine action because it is presumed to violate the natural laws of cause and effect. Divine action is seen as an "intervention" into an otherwise closed world of finite causality. Doing or acting is something that is for human beings alone (although some might include animals) because it is what finite, not infinite, realities do. Doing is structured, conditioned, or restricted by the conditions of the STMW. (Though, as we shall see, the strictures of scientific causality are such that in many scientific views even human action is impossible if it presupposes freedom of choice, a freedom which strict mechanistic determinism rules out.) God, it is assumed, must have a nature that is so radically different, or what philosophers call "ontologically other" (that is, God's very being—God's "ontos"—is so absolutely transcendent of the STMW that constitutes our finite human "ontos," our essential being that "he" cannot act in the world as we act in it). At the very least we have no conceptual categories or language to reflect what it is *that* God "does," let alone *how* God acts. At its very best the concept of "doing" or acting can only be attributed to God non-literally and non-directly, that is, in a way that is radically different from the way in which we attribute it to ourselves as personal agents.

Given the paucity of human language and the need of the religious practitioner to believe that she is in touch with a Someone not absolutely and completely different from herself, this Someone is usually described in personal terms. That is why the pronoun "someone" is religiously more resonant than the word "something." Even those philosophers of religion who assiduously insist that God is not, in God's own self, a personal agent, still tend to use personal language when referring to God. Partly this is a consequence of language itself, which has either personal or impersonal pronouns. It also presupposes subject-object distinctions. But it has seemed the better part of discretion, or sensitivity to religious inclinations, even while denying the literal use of personal agent-language for God, to refer to God using a personal pronoun without actually assuming that God is, in Godself, a personal agent.

The word "God" is widely used and invoked in the major monotheistic traditions: Judaism, Christianity, and Islam. There is probably no word in the religious vocabulary of these traditions that evokes more contention, confusion, and concern in the areas of philosophy and theology than the one that refers to what is variously called God, Yahweh, Adonai, Elohim, Allah, Jehovah, Lord of Hosts, Creator, the Holy One, One without a second, Supreme Being, Being-Itself, Ground of Being, Act of Being, or Wholly Other. Even when not being used in philosophical and theological debates, "God" is a word often used as a placeholder for an often inchoate, even inexplicable sense of a reality that is intrinsically mysterious because it is other and greater than human beings and the material, spatial, and temporal world they occupy.

But so what? Why do people care about the meaning reflected in or pointed to by the word "God" and its various synonyms? The fact is that many religious practitioners do care and care passionately. This passion is found equally among those viscerally hostile to religious belief as well as those deeply invested in such belief. And the reason is that "God" in and of Godself is either a reality who makes a decisive difference in the living of meaningful lives, or God is a non-reality, and belief in whom has been pernicious, baleful, and the cause of immense human suffering as well as being a crippling and destructive delusion. Either way, both believers and detractors view God or the concept of God with deadly seriousness. Passionate atheists are often closer to the heart of religious sensibility than are people who don't think about God at all.

So getting clear about the concept of God will be central to a healthy debate between religious and non-religious believers. If there is to be a genuine debate, as opposed to ill-informed mudslinging on both sides of the God-belief controversy, the object of that debate needs to be clearly identified. Too often, attacks on God-belief assume one notion of God while defenders of a God-belief assume a very different notion. This often means that the opponents are simply talking past one another. One needs only to look at the intelligent design versus evolution controversy to see a contemporary example.

From the side of religious believers in the theistic tradition, there are a variety of religious practices in which reference to God is far less contentious and theologically problematic than it is in the world of philosophical and theological reflection on the utilization of God-language. In the prayers and liturgies of these traditions, God is not the subject of theological debate but is assumed to be not the abstract product of metaphysical thought, but instead a palpable, living, and personal reality to whom people offer prayers, intercessions, thanksgivings, and praise, and from whom they expect a variety of responses, from answering prayers to physical and psychological healing. And those engaging in these religious activities are not at all troubled by the implicit (and sometimes quite explicit) reference to a particular kind of God, namely God as a personal agent whose actions have made and continue to make a decisive difference in the lives and histories of human beings and the world. Only a God who can *make a difference* in the world in the lives of persons is worthy of worship.

A God who is *only* a completely transcendent reality beyond the conceptual reach of human beings is not relevant to religious life even though such a God may satisfy certain speculative or conceptual urges among the super-philosophical. But if God is to make a *practical* difference in the lives of persons, God must somehow act in, respond to, or otherwise make a difference for them. If God is to make a difference, religious practitioners need a coherent concept of God to make sense of their liturgical and scriptural references to God. In liturgy, prayer and scripture, God is depicted as making a decisive historical difference in the lives of God's people, both collectively and individually. God calls, sends, rebukes, covenants, inspires, leads, speaks, rescues, demands, transforms, and so on. In short, God "delivers"; God is the active deliverer (from sin, injustice, oppression, meaninglessness, disease, etc.). But all forms of deliverance require divine acts, which are, as such, historically and personally decisive. Only if we establish the primordiality of God as an agent can we intelligibly discuss *the modes of divine action* or *how* God acts. There is an enormous amount of literature that has been developed by scholars trying to explain the modes of God's action in a way that does not conflict with a scientific understanding of the doings and behaviors that constitute the STMW. We will examine them only after we have established the ground for first thinking of God as a primordially personal agent.

In the scriptures or holy writings of the three monotheistic traditions, God is consistently spoken of as or presumed to be an agent in the same basic sense that human beings are agents: God performs actions and responds to the actions of the human persons as one agent among others in a common field of action. God creates, sustains, commands, affirms, punishes, empowers, sends, inspires, reveals, and even speaks, as only agents can do (as opposed to things that are nothing more than biological organisms and material objects). Only agents can perform acts[6] and the Bible is sometimes referred to as the Book of the Acts of God. Verbs, not nouns, are the primary, basic, and appropriate way by which God is described because they articulate *what God does*. *Who God is* is revealed only through divine actions.

If one remained at the level of liturgical language, these references to God acting would be relatively unproblematic. Religious believers in the monotheistic religions gather to remember the acts of God: the creation of the world; the calling of Abraham; the rescue of the Israelites in Egypt; the giving of a covenant to them at Mt. Sinai; the miraculous interventions in their occupation of the land of Palestine, such as the parting of the waters of the Red Sea; the sending of the prophets; the calling and commissioning of Mohammed; and, for Christians, the incarnation of Jesus, his resurrection from the dead, and the sending of the Holy Spirit.

But when one moves from liturgical to theological/philosophical language about God, one enters much more troubled and contentious waters regarding the meaning of the term "God" and especially the concept of God as an agent. The concepts of agency and the agents who act clearly apply to human beings. We know ourselves primarily as agents who act. In fact, knowing is itself an act that we perform in order to get a better handle on the world in which we are agent-participants. We cannot escape being agents or knowing ourselves

---

6. This is why the concepts of agency, act, action, and agent are all interrelated and why each entails the others, though personal agency is the basis for thinking about all the others.

primordially as agents because agency is presupposed in every conscious thought we have and every action we perform. Even the moments of mental withdrawal from the busyness of our everyday lives are the result of an intentional act performed so as to attain a state of contemplation. We withdraw from one kind of action by another act (of thinking) in order to reflect on our previous actions. (We also know that there are many things in which, through our bodies, we are intimately implicated that are not acts: the beating of my heart is not an act of mine, nor is my being swept away by a wave, but I am deeply implicated, or at least my body is, in both of these events.) But when I deliberately run fast in order to get my heart to beat faster, that is an act since I am doing something intentionally to bring about a particular material result. In short, I am an agent but not everything that occurs in and through me is an act of mine. But without the capacity to act (i.e., without intentionality and the ability to form conscious purposes, such as when I fall into a coma), I am less than the full person I can be.

Many philosophers and theologians consider action performed by human beings, and the consequent understanding of action as that which human agents do, inappropriate for describing the kind of action God performs. The assumption underlying this inappropriateness is that God is radically unlike human beings. There is, it is assumed, a complete and absolute difference (sometimes called an ontological difference to highlight its utter difference from everything else) between whatever is human, and therefore finite and limited, and whatever God is and does. And since agency is clearly the right concept for understanding what we ourselves are and do as agents, it cannot be applied to God in any literal, direct, or unqualified way—or so the argument goes.

According to the view that God cannot literally be an agent, there are multiple limitations on the direct, literal, or unqualified use of the concept of agent when applied by philosophers and theologians to God. Agents exist within a common field of others that also includes non-agents: agents have objects external to themselves upon which they act and are, technically speaking, limited and conditioned by those other realities. The dualist theological tradition assumes that God is beyond or transcendent of any limitations or conditions imposed by anything outside Godself. This dualist tradition is based on the metaphysical principle of the utter ontological otherness or transcendence of God.

I want to argue that, contrary to dualism, it will be impossible to make sense of the liturgical language of the worshipping communities of the monotheistic religions without conceiving of God as a personal agent. Without this conception, it will also be impossible to make sense of their scriptural references to God's role in history and nature. The liturgical practices of faithful Jews, Christians, Muslims, and other theists are grounded (whether their practitioners are aware of this or not) in a philosophically defensible metaphysical view of reality in which God is, in fact, a personal agent. The language of these liturgical practices as well as the language of their scriptures or holy writings also presupposes this metaphysical view and concept of God. I want to show how the notion of God as agent can be given coherent and persuasive support by mining the full implications of notions of agency, act, and agent.

GOD AS A PERSONAL AGENT: DISPUTED POINTS

Adopting a view of God as personal agent brings both virtues and vices in its wake. In addition to the "vice" of anthropomorphism, there is the problem that if God is an agent, God becomes inextricably implicated in evil since God has the capacity to act in the world so as to eradicate or at least mitigate it. Non-agent divine beings that cannot act (because their transcendent nature makes such action inconceivable or because they are "beyond" action) cannot be held accountable for not abolishing evil, but an agent God presumably can be.

A third downside to the concept of God as agent is the difficulty of determining, with a reasonable degree of certainty, exactly what God *has in fact done*. If God can be shown to be metaphysically *able* to act in the world, then what actions turn out to be uniquely God's and which are not? And how do we tell the difference?

A fourth problem is that this view runs smack into the claims of contemporary scientific explanation. If the scientific worldview presumes that all occurrences in the world, including those we have traditionally thought of as belonging to free personal agents, can be subsumed under a causally reductive and exhaustive explanatory scheme that has no room for free agency of any kind, then it will conflict with a view of God as an agent. This conflict is presently being exemplified in the intelligent design versus evolution debate. One defense some religious believers have made to what they consider excessive claims of intelligent design is to deny that God intervenes or interferes in any way at all with the natural, causal processes of the world. This is, I will argue, too high a price to pay for a rapprochement between science and religion. However, adopting a view of God as a personal agent does not necessarily entail a direct confrontation with scientific understanding, especially if the latter does not claim to be reductionistically *exhaustive* in its explanation of everything that happens in the world. Its explanatory scheme might well apply to all non-intentional, non-personal occurrences without being able to cover those things that are genuinely free acts by intentional personal agents. The world that science explores is the infrastructure that agents utilize in carrying out their intentions and, as infrastructure, does not threaten the primordiality of the agent who utilizes it.

A fifth area of concern regarding the concept of God as agent is its apparent inability to satisfy the human craving for ultimate mystery. A God who is too easily known or whose nature and revelatory acts are too accessible to the human mind through its normal cognitive powers, threatens some of the mysterious, supersensible dimensions of God that many people seem to believe must be present in any acceptable theism. I will want to argue that a view of God as personal agent actually restores an *appropriate* sense of mystery to God: not one that is intrinsically supernatural or supersensible, but one that belongs to agents as such: the mystery of freedom; the mystery of personality; the mystery that inheres in any free personal being capable of outdistancing our scientific predictions or causal explanations of them. It is more appropriate, I will argue, to locate mystery in personality rather than in abstract philosophical concepts derived from the belief that the only genuine mystery lies entirely outside or "under" the universe.

The virtue of the view of God as personal agent is that it makes sense of the scriptural, liturgical, personal-prayer, and personal-experience language about God. Persons in the theistic traditions encounter God in a variety of ways, including the rehearsal of God's acts in history and the personal experience of the presence of God in moments of inspiration, healing, comfort, and reassurance. Only language of God as agent can make sense of these encounters and experiences. The concept also coheres well with a specific metaphysical view. It brings God within the range of human conceptuality and undergirds an understanding of how and why God can make a difference in the world and in the lives of its inhabitants. And if there are freely intended and performed actions by personal agents in the world, God will be one of those agents (though suitably and appropriately differentiated from them because of the reach of God's power, steadfastness of purpose, captiousness, and grace-filled love) whose acts make all the difference to the lives of persons with whom God interacts. Another virtue is the obverse of the implication of God in the problem of evil: precisely because God *can* act to deal with evil, God's actions become essential to its overcoming. God can deliver on the divine promise to bring all persons to fulfillment by interfering in the world to combat evil. If God's intention is to overcome evil and restore a broken creation, then prayers for such deliverance begin to make sense. So does the imperative to align oneself with those divine actions that intend to overcome oppression and injustice because one will be placing oneself in the continuity of divine and human action tending toward the completion of God's intentions for the world.

Even if one does adopt a notion of divine agency, however, there are numerous and often quite different theological understandings of *how* God acts in the world. I want to examine these in order to place my view that God not only acts generally and universally to create and sustain the whole STMW but also acts discretely and particularly *within* the STMW; in other words, God performs some acts that are uniquely God's own, alongside the acts of other agents and non-agent causality. These alternative views of the "how" of God's action in the world range from the deistic (God creates the universe and lets it run itself without further interference) to the most fundamentalist (God is the agent who directly causes *every* occurrence as recorded in Scripture, including the creation of the world 6,000 years ago.) Some of the different understandings of divine action are compatible with each other under the concept of divine agency that I will adopt and some are not. I will explore in some detail these areas of compatibility and incompatibility.

The most problematic aspect of most accounts of divine action revolves around the concept of divine "intervention" or "interference" in the structures of the world. It is assumed that such interference or intervention will violate the scientific causal understanding of how the events of the world are to be construed. Most attempts to explain divine action are developed subsequently so as to avoid any reference to divine interference. My argument will be that in some sense *all* agents *necessarily* interfere with or intervene in what would be, without their presence, an *otherwise* closed causal web of events (closed, that is to free action by agents). But I will also argue that "interference," while metaphysically acceptable in some basic sense, is not as good as the notion of "utilization" or deployment, which turns the notion of the primacy of the causal nexus on its head. Actions, I will argue, do not need to fit into the causal nexus precisely because they transcend it by being able to use it as the infrastructure through which the intentions of the agent are realized. Interference is appropriate in one sense, however, because without agent interference, the scientific explanation is appropriately complete and exhaustive. But if free personal agents exist and act, their acts intrude upon, intervene in, subsume, or interfere with that closed causal web. If the web is absolutely, without remainder, complete and exhaustive, then there is no such thing as freely enacted intentions. But if acts that are brought about by free agents do occur, then the closed causal web is not exhaustive of *everything* that happens, only of those things that are not agent initiated. An act, however, while interfering with or intervening in the web, does not necessarily *violate* the causal principles or natural laws that explain non-agent caused events. (I do not want to rule out the possibility, perhaps rare, that some divine actions may entail a superceding or *transgression* of the laws of nature, but such transgressions are not required for divine action to take place.) Actions may supervene upon or utilize the causal factors in the closed web without violating its causal infrastructure. In fact, as I shall argue, they deploy or utilize that infrastructure in the attainment of their ends and this notion of the deployment of the causal infrastructure avoids the worst misinterpretations found in the notion of interference. (A common example, the full meaning of which I will develop, is that by choosing to supervene upon the causal factors that normally produce the unconscious and unintended blinking of my eyelids, I can bring about a more rapid or slower blinking of my eyelids. In doing so, I am not contravening the laws of nature, but instead *utilizing* the causal infrastructure for an intention it does not itself initiate. It is appropriate, I believe, to continue to think of this utilization as an interference as long as the latter notion does not presume that my action must "fit into" the causal structure.) If this example is successfully mined, it can provide an overarching explanatory scheme in which God utilizes the laws of nature (without violating them) to accomplish divine ends. But such utilization is not inconsistent with an appropriately understood notion of intervention and interference as would apply to any act that is not solely the result of causal laws or forces. The full explication of this notion will constitute the heart of my argument for the virtue of a view of God as a personal agent.

Conclusion

Ultimately, what I hope to achieve is the development of a coherent, metaphysically sound argument for the notion of God as a personal agent who can actually act *in* the world in discrete and particular ways in addition to sustaining by a "master" act the entire structure of the world. I believe that such a notion will support the use of the language about God found in the liturgies, scriptures, prayer life, and personal experience of most people in the theistic traditions. It will give faithful practitioners of the theistic traditions a metaphysical leg to stand on and allow them to make sense of the language they employ in their prayers, creeds, scriptures, and liturgies. It will reconcile some of the many tensions that have emerged when, in addition to agent language about God, the theological traditions felt compelled to also employ the language of ontological transcendence or undifferentiated oneness. In the process, it will restore to health a view of God that philosophers and theologians have too often discarded as too anemic or naïve (too anthropomorphic) to do justice to the religious life and personal relations with God.

I want to think from the primordiality of the notion of agency and on that basis find a place for other ways of conceiving or symbolizing God. Most approaches to God think from the primordiality of something else: something so ontologically "other" that agency becomes at best only a metaphor or symbol for God but not reflective of God's essential being. I want to reverse this way of approaching God. I believe that the essential character of agency (and its metaphysically correlative notions of self, agent, and person) *is* the essential character of God and, when mined sensitively, carries within it all that the liturgical, prayerful, and personal approaches to God intend or need.

1

Otherness and Oneness
Rival Conceptions of God

The twin desires for a personal God and a transcendent God, a God who is in the deepest possible relationship with me and a God who is not limited by relating to something "less" than God has led many thinkers in three different directions in forming a concept of God. One is toward what some have dismissively called an anthropomorphic view of God (ontological pluralism) in which God is pictured as something like a human being (though greater by degree). A second is toward ontological monism, or a mystical understanding of the divine reality that erases the distinctions between God and "others" by annihilating the ontological status of difference between these others and God and leaves only undifferentiated oneness. The third, ontological dualism, is a view of God as absolutely "other" and ontologically transcendent of everything other than the divine self. (I will argue that this third view of God, dualism, eventually collapses into the view [monism] that erases all distinctions, including the one of transcendence, between God and everything else.) Having developed a qualified rejection of the second two views, I will return to the ontological pluralism view, but on what I believe are deeper, more satisfying metaphysical grounds than those associated with a primitive anthropomorphism and that are built around the primordial concept of personal agency.

Ontological Dualism or Radical Difference

Let us begin with ontological dualism, the drive toward Otherness and Radical Transcendence, before examining the mystical move toward ontological monism.

Much of western theism is characterized by an insistence on the complete and absolute "otherness" of God from anything that is not God. "Otherness" is a term of art intended to reflect the conviction that whatever God is—in and of Godself—God must be absolutely, ontologically, or essentially *other than* or *different from* everything that is not-God. Some philosophers call this the "alterity" of God. Some theologians, such as Karl Barth, call God the "Wholly Other." (The failure to settle on a single term for this phenomenon is due in large part to the paucity of language, a paucity that flows naturally from the premises of dualism. All speech is grounded in our experiences within the finite world and to use such speech to talk about something which is not part of that world is inherently problematic and paradoxical.) Assumedly, to be truly God, God cannot be *part of* or a participant in a reality greater than Godself because that would condition or limit God's being, at least in some respects, upon or in relation to the world with which God is in relationship. The very notion of "relationship" is fraught with problems for those insisting on radical otherness precisely because relationship entails some kind of continuity or commonality between those "beings" that stand in relation to each other.

We will use the word *world* in this context to refer to the totality of all real things and the conditions necessary for their existence. The world we inhabit, the world whose conditions apply to "us," in this sense, is the totality of space, time, and matter (STMW). In religious terminology it is often called simply "the finite" or "finitude" to contrast it with what is not finite, or the infinite. ("*Infinite*" means simply *not* finite, and many claim that it is impossible to ever say what the not-finite really is precisely because it is not finite and we can only think and articulate in concepts drawn from and limited to the finite.) Monotheists assume that God, to be God, must somehow be responsible for as either the creator or origin of this finite totality without being *in* or part *of* it. God must, in some sense, be *outside of* or radically *other than* the world while remaining, in some mysterious sense, related to it as its creator and sustainer.

But the notion of "outside" or "other than" is tricky and conceptually problematic. To say that God is outside the world or other than the world necessarily presupposes that there is something Other than God. And if the "world" is other than God, doesn't its otherness qualify the fullness or absolute self-sufficiency of God's reality taken in and of itself? It certainly limits God (at least some people believe this to be the case) by restricting God from *being* this "other" reality that is not God. God cannot "be" finite and still be God, which raises the question of what ontological status does that which is not God have in relation to God? Clearly the finite exists since it forms the foundation for the first attempts to think of God as "other" than the finite. But the tendency to think beyond otherness begins here, because the second option (ontological monism) referred to above promises to resolve the question of how something can be other than God without compromising the absoluteness of God by subsuming that non-divine reality *into* divinity, so that otherness itself ultimately disappears. If God *is* the totality of an undifferentiated single reality, then God is not "other" than it and the totality needs no explanation from "outside" itself since there is no outside, by definition, of a totality. But if God is other than the world then God must account for, explain, or somehow cause to be (without literally being a cause in any kind of worldly sense) the entirety of the STMW and this means that God cannot be an object or being *within* that world. That means that God must be radically other than the world.

It is this otherness of God that the word "transcendent" is normally meant to reflect when it is applied to God. The problem, of course, is that the more God is made transcendent or other than the world the less God can be understood as having a relationship or connection with the world to which God stands as radically "other." If some kind of relationship with the Ultimate or divine reality is part of the religious aspiration, then emphasizing the divine Otherness is going to become extremely problematic because a relationship between two different beings or entities presupposes something common between them, some common ground in which they both exist and which makes the relationship between them possible. But otherness, alterity, or transcendence want to deny the common ground between God and what is other than God since placing God on the same ontological ground compromises God's transcendence of that ground. If God exists, God's very existence annihilates or cancels the reality of that which is not God. If God is radically or ontologically other than everything finite, and if I am finite, there is no common ground between us, thus annulling the possibility of a relationship between us.

Now, in western theism, the otherness of God is tied closely to what has been called the "classical" view of God. God is held to be transcendent of the world and is characterized as omnipotent, omniscient, immutable, immaterial, and eternal. (Many philosophers have argued that these terms do not attribute qualities directly or positively to God but instead deny God qualities extracted from and more properly attributed to beings *within* the world that God is said to transcend. This is sometimes called "negative" theology.) In this form of classical theology, God is not limited in power and knowledge, is not subject to space, change or mutation, is not material, and is not temporal (i.e., does not exist, persist, or endure "through" time. When God is called eternal it normally means existing beyond or outside of temporal duration). Negative theology, by denying human predicates to God, does not claim to know what God is "in God's own self," only what God is not. God's transcendence is "ontological" and is not to be confused with the kind of transcendence that is more loosely used in trying to compare a being of superlative degree to an inferior being with "less" of what is being attributed to God. The power of the king far transcends the power of the king's servant. But this kind of transcendence is transcendence by degree and is not radical or ontological. Only when the very essence or being of something is radically different from or other than something else can we say that it stands in a relation of ontological transcendence to it. This is a relation of course, that is not a "real" relation except in a stretched metaphorical sense since a completely ontologically transcendent God stands in no "relation" to anything other than Godself without compromising God's transcendence and otherness. This is another way of pointing to the difficulty any conception of a relationship with God has under the rubric of radical divine otherness or alterity. As we will see, one attempt to resolve the difficulty is to say that God has no relationship with us, but that we have a relationship with God because we *participate* in God as the ground of our being. This claim is, I believe, tantamount to identifying us and everything else *with* God and more appropriately falls into the monistic model of undifferentiated oneness. Of course, the temptation is to attempt to attenuate the radicality of otherness and simply concede that God must be like us in some general respects. That at least will resituate God back into a place where we share some ontological ground and thus can be related. But this move is fatal if one wants to avoid anthropomorphism or bringing God "back down" into the reach of human concepts and experiences. And it points to the dilemma around which this study is predicated: how to relate to God religiously in a way that fulfills my being as a human person and how to speak of God in a way that fulfills my desire to make God as mysterious as possible out of a fear of domesticating God by making the relationship with God too much dependent on my retaining my individual human being with all its inadequacies and limitations.

Pseudo-Dionysius

The difficulty of speaking about a being that ontologically transcends our (finite and conditioned) being has led some theologians to claim that speech about God is logically impossible. Pseudo-Dionysius the Areopagite (or Ps.-D, for short), a late fifth and earlysixth century Christian writer whose influence on medieval theology was significant, suggested that we have to take the position that language about the ontologically transcendent God is *apophatic*, that is, literally ineffable, unspeakable, or unsayable. Ps.-D reflects the classic Christian conundrum: a felt need to speak about God and an equally strong conviction that no speech about God is ever appropriate since God, given God's radical alterity, cannot be reflected or represented in human speech. Denys Turner has captured the paradoxical nature of Ps.-D's apophatic language about God when he calls it "that speech about God which is the failure of speech."[1] A key concept of Ps.-D, as rephrased by Paul Rorem, is the transcendence of knowledge: "since human knowledge is of beings, God who transcends being must also transcend our knowledge."[2] In a way that anticipates Thomas Aquinas, Ps.-D says "and so it is that as Cause of all and as transcending all,[3] he is rightly nameless and yet has the names of everything that is."[4] Ps.-D acknowledges that theology at times speaks of God "sometimes without, sometimes with distinctions."[5] The "all" to which God gives rise is differentiated and these differentiations begin with the "processions" out of or from God, the origination of the plurality of beings. How God does this is not clear and can only be expressed by way of metaphor (e.g., God's fullness of Being *overflows* itself and the overflow becomes the world of multiplicity and difference, both between the beings that constitute the world and between God and those beings taken both individually and as a whole). Even though they proceed or emanate from God and even though God's being must somehow "inform" or ground them, they remain differentiated and distinct from God (otherwise they would *be* fully divine themselves and the ontological distinction between God and what is not God would be lost. Finally accepting the logic of this fact will lead ultimately to ontological monism).

Ps.-D even argues that negative theological terms such as ineffability, unknowability, and the transcendence of all finite assertions are, strictly speaking, not applicable to God. God is beyond both positive and negative attribution. Creation becomes a "form of differentiation" in a neo-platonic sense. All things differentiated from their source ultimately participate in God as their source. God, however, is not diminished or emptied by their emanation from God; "He remains one amid the plurality, united throughout the procession, and full amid the emptying act of differentiation."[6] God is not

---

1. Denys Turner, *The Darkness of God* (Cambridge: Cambridge University Press, 1995), 20. Language about God is ultimately "the collapse of our affirmation and denials into disorder, which we can only express, *a fortiori*, in bits of collapsed, disordered language . . ." (22).

2. Paul Rorem, *Pseudo-Dionysius* (New York: Oxford University Press, 1993), 136.

3. This claim does not explain how something that is radically "other" can be a cause if the meaning of "cause" is derived from that which is caused. See John Morreall, *Analogy and Talking About God: A Critique of the Thomistic Approach* (Washington, DC: University Press of America, 1979).

4. Rorem, *Pseudo-Dionysius*, 137.

5. Ibid., 138.

6. Ibid., 144.

differentiated, but the beings that flow from the overabundance of God are differentiated both from each other and from God while at the same time remaining ontologically grounded in God. (Note how close to ontological monism is Ps.-D's ostensible ontological dualism: there is differentiation, but it hovers over non-differentiation.) We have clearly entered the realm of linguistic paradox here, but paradox is the inevitable result of trying to use the language that presupposes differentiation (e.g., between subject and object, predicates applied to things, nouns, verbs, etc.) to work at all in order to speak of non-differentiation and unity in God.

Ultimately, Ps.-D argues that it is only by ceasing to be oneself or anything else, that one becomes "supremely united to the completely unknown [God] by the inactivity of all knowledge, and known beyond the mind by knowing nothing."[7] This may seem completely nonsensical and unintelligible. How can one claim to be united to that which is completely unknown (unless one has some knowledge of that to which one is united even though the union is itself beyond knowledge and comprehension)? How is knowing by knowing nothing any form of knowing at all? Whatever the limitations of knowledge, knowing has certain characteristics such as the cognitive or mental conceptualization of some object or thing (from which the concept of it is distinguished or differentiated). Knowing nothing is either paradoxical, perhaps a literary way of saying that one does not know *certain things* about an object, or it is meaningless. Knowledge is always intentional (as that term is drawn from phenomenology, not from the philosophy of action): it has an object about which it can conceptually grasp something and articulate that something in differentiating language. But one winds up in these conundrums as soon as one insists that God is radically "other" and ontologically transcendent and at the same time insists that finite thinkers have some cognitive access to God despite God's radical otherness. Ps.-D says at one point in his writings:

> Since God is a 'being' in a way beyond being, he bestows existence upon everything and brings the whole world into being, so that his single existence is said [in human language] to be manifold by virtue of the fact that it brings so many things to being from itself. Yet he remains one, nothing less than himself. He remains one amid the plurality, united throughout the procession, and full amid the emptying act of differentiation.[8]

---

7. Ibid., 192.
8. Pseudo-Dionysius, *The Divine Names*. Qtd. in Rorem, *Pseudo-Dionysius*, 144.

God is said elsewhere to have "turned outward to differentiation"[9] through a procession from Godself. Clearly differentiation is "other than" God, something below or less than God (though how thorough or absolute that otherness is, is not entirely clear). And yet it is only through differentiation that we acquire the capacity of language and, thereby, the words with which to refer to God who is beyond differentiation. And because words arise from the world of differentiation they are ultimately inappropriately applied to God if applied without qualification since differentiation is other than God. In discussing Ps.-D, Turner focuses on language—not on the concept of God, per se. He is acutely conscious of the paradoxical nature of language about the divine. In this context, Turner reminds us not to consider "difference" between God and everything else as something that can be articulated.

> "Difference" and "similarity" are terms which are themselves infinitely deficient in describing features of our language about God. We cannot say what God is because we cannot express what that degree of difference is which falls between what we can say of God and what God is. We know that our language about God fails. But we have no language about our language about God which can adequately describe the extent of the failure of our descriptions."[10]

Sometimes Ps.-D contrasts the darkness of unknowing (in which no differentiation appears because the dark hides all of it) with the light of knowledge. In this respect darkness, the absence of light is superior to the light that illuminates differentiation.

At any rate Dionysius holds that all attributes are differentiations and technically speaking cannot apply to God who is not a being but standing in differentiated relationship with other beings. Only by creation, or more properly by emanation flowing from God, does differentiation *between* beings become in some sense "real," though not ultimately real since no single being or the multitude or totality of beings can ever have complete ontological independence from God. Creation is, in effect, differentiation and differentiation is not an attribute of God prior to creation. (This means, incidentally, that what Christians call the Incarnation, God becoming flesh, is impossible to understand on the basis of ontological dualism or, as it turns out, on ontological monism as well, which may well be why Karl Barth rejects all forms of humanly originated thinking as a way of understanding God.)

---

9. Ibid.
10. Turner, *The Darkness of God*, 43.

Now if the difference or otherness that characterizes God is absolute, God will have no connection with the world. But this absence of any connection eliminates the possibility of thinking of God as the *creator* of what is not Godself. As David Burrell has put it, if we try to think of God as absolutely other, then we cannot use the name "creator" for God or make "divinity in any way accessible to our discourse."[11] Discourse, or speaking about something, referring to something, or making a claim about something, presupposes some differentiation between the speaker and that about which he or she is speaking. Language, in short, only works on the assumption that there are differences between beings or objects in the world to which the speaker is referring. Nouns distinguish one object from another. Adjectives apply to nouns that refer to objects. Now all of this is pretty straightforward until one comes to the problem of speaking about God. If God is not an object *in* the world (as most philosophers who lean toward this way of thinking would agree), then no word whose meaning is originally derived from our experience of objects in the world can refer, without qualification or straightforwardly, to that which is not and cannot be experienced as existing or being in the world. But if God absolutely transcends the world (is not contained in or qualified by any of the conditions that constitute the world), then no word whose origin is from the world can refer to God directly or without qualification. This is obviously true, as we shall see more fully in our treatment of ontological monism, if God is the undifferentiated unity of all "things" (things being in some sense unreal if they are regarded as ontologically distinct from each other). But it is also true if God is the absolutely "other" who transcends the world.

It is not enough simply to assert God's radical ontological transcendence or otherness because, as Burrell notes, we thereby lose any contact with God if we are that in comparison to which God is transcendent. On the other hand, it is also not possible to assert God's total presence to us without implying that God is not more or other than us, thinking of God as not totally transcendent but as totally immanent: as an omni-presence, as present to everything that constitutes reality. But being "present to" means present to what is not the divine self or being completely self-present, present only to Godself as containing all things, there being no distinction between God and that which is at first glance seemingly "other" than God. This is another way of stating the difference between ontological dualism and ontological monism and, at the same time, their incredible closeness. Each is an attempt to preserve the mystery of God, to extricate God from the STMW, but without completely losing contact with

---

11. David Burrell, *Knowing the Unknowable God: Ibn-Sina, Maimonides, Aquinas* (Notre Dame, IN: University of Notre Dame Press, 1986), 17.

God. Without contact, connection, or relationship of some kind, the religious motive for desiring God will be completely extinguished even though it may achieve a certain kind of cognitive satisfaction by having pushed beyond the limits of thought entirely and thereby preserved, in its own way, the absolute mystery of God even at the cost of the meaningfulness of language and the annihilation of thought about God.

To be mysterious, God must be different from us. But the primordial problem for theology and philosophy is just how to articulate that difference in any kind of language whose very condition of meaning is some basic similarity or commonness between the speaker and the object about which he or she speaks, when that object is God.

If God is absolutely other, no words drawn from the reality in comparison to which God is other will ever suffice. If God is absolutely present or immanent, not distinguishable from the totality of all beings that constitute reality, no words can refer to God since reference requires differentiation and distinction among the beings of reality.

No wonder Dionysius's apophatic approach has become so popular. It is tantamount to denying the ability to speak rationally about something, while making the denial in such a way that the subject is actually referred to as precisely that which is not rationally conceptualizable. By saying that God is not finite, one is not describing God (the word "infinite" simply means not finite), but one is conveying *something* meaningful by denying that God is a being within or part of the STMW. That seems to say *something* about God (i.e., that God is absolutely "other") without saying exactly in what God's otherness consists or how to refer to the "content" of that otherness.

John Scotus Erigena

A clear example of negative theology after Ps.-D that continues his work can be found in the work of the ninth century Christian mystic John Scotus Erigena. In his work *The Division of Nature*, Erigena says that "we can no more express and comprehend His [God's] existence than we can the existence of nothingness. The terms *deus* and *nihil* are therefore logically equal: both express something beyond the pale of existence *as we know it* in the universe. . . . So it is in any doctrine of God: we are trying to name the Nameless." Erigena goes on to distinguish between metaphorical references and metaphysical references to God (which are those of "practical religion"). In metaphysics, metaphor is out of place, and "if we are to make any philosophic statements about God at all, they must be negative in form, that they may suggest a limitless positivity for which we have no other language."[12]

Emerich Coreth

A contemporary approach to the otherness of God (which also verges on monistic non-differentiation, a verge that ultimately becomes a merge as I will argue later) can be found in the work of some contemporary philosophers, sometimes associated with what is known as transcendental Thomism (from the work of Thomas Aquinas). This approach dismisses any notion of God as a singular being or individual *within* the ontological field that constitutes finitude. Instead, it wants to find God beyond that field as its presupposition, its horizon, or its ground. But as ground or horizon, God is not one being among many. God transcends all distinctions while not being distinct from anything other than Godself. God is, as Emerich Coreth puts it, beyond even the distinction of monism and dualism. In his book *Metaphysics*, Coreth investigates the very conditions of the possibility of knowledge and in the process discovers God as the ground or horizon of those conditions, even though God cannot be in or spoken of using language derived directly from those conditions.

Coreth insists that one cannot start from premises that are finite, contingent, and relative and arrive at that which is infinite, necessary, and absolute. Yet from one's ability to question one's finitude one already "knows" (though it is not ordinary knowledge) that there is something beyond the limits of those conditions. "To know a limit as limit is already to be beyond this limit."[13] And that which is beyond the limit is the horizon of being, an object (though not really an object in any sense in which that word is normally used), in the words of Joseph Donceel, "about which [one] can really say that it *is*, that it fully exhausts the fullness of this predicate. Only the Infinite comes up to this fullness, only God really *is*. All other objects are *this* or *that*."[14] Distinctions (what the ontological monists call differentiations) between one entity and another are endemic to finitude and the Absolute must transcend such distinctions. The infinite *is* what it is by not being differentiated from other objects whose differentiated nature is marked by "this-ness" or "that-ness"

---

12. Qtd. in Milton Munitz, *The Question of Reality* (Princeton, NJ: Princeton University Press, 1990), 63. The text from Erigena is from *De Divisione Naturae*, 643D in Henry Bett, *John Scotus Erigena* (Cambridge: Cambridge University Press, 1925; New York: Russell & Russell, 1964), 20. Citations refer to Russell edition.

13. Emerich Coreth, *Metaphysics* (New York: Seabury, 1973), 59.

14. Ibid., 11.

and with whom God would have stand "in relation" if God's difference from them is not absolute. Being is the unlimited horizon of everything.[15] Being is the condition for our thinking in the first place. Our interrogation of being presupposes that "only unconditioned, absolute being can put an end to our questioning."[16] In short, our very intellectual act of thinking about ourselves and our world brings to consciousness the unconditioned absolute being on which all intellectual acts—and our very existence as finite beings—depend. But this is not itself an "object" to be conceptually grasped through or by those acts.

Coreth claims that

> the dynamism of our intellect pushes irresistibly, although unthematically, past every finite being towards its ultimate ground, towards being as the unconditioned horizon. Hence the movement of our mind always intends absolute being. This striving, this finality is co-affirmed, as a condition of its possibility, in every act of thinking. And every single object, which is known as a being, is grasped as a partial end or goal, as a step towards unlimited being. It follows that every single being, as such, is essentially subordinated to absolute being, since it is used by our mind as a step or means towards it.[17]

Here Coreth is exploiting that sense of absolute mystery that always seems to hover at the edge of our religious sensibility. We simply cannot accept that the world we sense and think is all there is or explains itself in its own terms. There must be a ground on which it rests but that we cannot penetrate with the tools of ordinary thought and logic. The very uneasiness we feel at the limits of our thinking point beyond themselves to that which grounds them and which, in this way of thinking, is God.

The mysterious and radically "Other" toward which the mind is allegedly drawn[18] is absolutely unconditioned and infinite and thereby completely transcends the conditioned or finite. Coreth argues that "the mind's dynamism can reach the existent in its unconditioned validity only if it always anticipates the simply unconditioned; the intellectual dynamism, through which we grasp being in its unconditioned validity, is possible only on the basis of the

15. Ibid., 62.
16. Ibid., 64.
17. Ibid., 100.
18. I am not convinced that it is of the very essence of the human mind to be drawn to that which mysteriously transcends it. I can understand the attraction of intellectual mystery, but I am doubtful that it can form the basis for a coherent metaphysics in which God as a relational Other plays a vital part.

intellectual anticipation of the simply unconditioned within whose horizon we are able to know beings in their conditioned unconditionality."[19] Furthermore, "the dynamism of our mind proceeds necessarily beyond every finite object, beyond the sum of all possible finite objects, towards the infinite itself. It can reach its fulfillment only in the unlimited. But the unlimited towards which our dynamism keeps striving . . . is not an infinity within finiteness; for such an infinite would still be potential infinity within actual finiteness. It is an infinity *before* or *above* all the finite; for only in this way can it exist as actual infinity, that is, as the real fullness of all the infinite possibilities of being."[20]

This approach to the "otherness" of God preserves God in a way that highlights the mystery of the divine reality without completely severing the link between God and the rest of reality. That link is the intellectual dynamism of the mind that presupposes the divine in and through its intellectual acts. It is not clear whether this link is sufficient to placate those of us who want a *relationship* with a divine being that fulfills our whole nature or whether it places God simply too far beyond not only our conceptual reach but also beyond our psycho-social need for relationality with respect to non-cognitive dimensions of our being.

But difference is not the last word for Coreth. He tries to close the gap between absolute otherness and undifferentiated oneness in a way that anticipates the work of radical mysticism or ontological monism, reminiscent of Meister Eckhart and W.T. Stace (whose work we will examine next). He does so by insisting that absolute being is the first origin of all the multiplicity and diversity of the finite beings, and that it must contain "absolute identity" and at the same time "difference or non-identity." "This difference must be such that it does not introduce into the absolute positivity any negativity which might render the infinite finite, the absolute relative."[21]

So there must be posited in the unity of absolute being a "relative opposition, on account of which there may originate in it the essence of the finite existent."[22] How this happens (and why) is ultimately unexplained by Coreth, as is the notion of "relative opposition." But he reaffirms the absolute otherness of God by reminding us that absolute being "cannot itself be an object within this horizon."[23] This is the limitation of being presupposed by finite being. If we abstract from this limitation we "get once more concepts of

---

19. Ibid., 173.
20. Ibid., 174.
21. Ibid., 89.
22. Ibid., 101.
23. Ibid., 116.

pure being, which contain no more limit and lead our minds toward infinity. Since all these concepts are without limit, they are no longer separated from other similar concepts. They coincide one with another and apply to the one unlimited reality, absolute being."[24] And, echoing the apophasis of Ps.-D, he says that they apply to absolute being "eminently, in a manner which exceeds infinitely the manner in which they apply to finite beings" and thus are presumably beyond all human understanding. "Absolute being is pure self-presence of being with itself. It is therefore absolute spirit."[25]

Nevertheless, God remains absolutely other to us. "Since it [God] is not a being among beings, not an object within the horizon of possible objects, it can never directly in itself become an object of knowledge, the absolute cannot be represented or conceived in the way of a being."[26] This would seem to rule out any notion of God as a being in relation to us.

Absolute being is infinite, simple, immutable, supra-temporal, and supra-spatial. The absolute is not identical with "but different from and transcendent with respect to all finite beings. It is the infinitely other, infinitely exceeding all finite beings, never entering immanently into them, but forever remaining transcendent as the pure actuality of being."[27]

Given all this, it is interesting that Coreth tries to find a place in his metaphysical view for action. Absolute being, he argues, is "fully self-identical, self-identified, self-identity, and this . . . is the supremely pure form of *activity*. It is an activity which implies no change, no passage from one state to another. It is activity that is identical with absolute being, it is infinitely perfect self-subsistent activity. *It is an activity which does not reach out to another being*, since the infinite being cannot actuate itself in another, in a finite being."[28] This means, of course, that such a being cannot act in the primordial sense of the term: this notion of activity is a reduction from or a very different use of the notion of act from the one we normally use in referring to agents in the world. It implies non-differentiation within infinite being and not an action between

24. Ibid., 117.
25. Ibid., 118.
26. Ibid., 182.
27. Ibid., 185.
28. Ibid.186. Emphasis added. This is reminiscent of the Aristotelian/Thomistic understanding of "act" as the lack of potentiality in a being. Act is the completion or fulfillment of being and thus, in a sense, is the opposite of what we normally mean by act, which implies that the agent "acts" in order to attain something of which he or she presently is not in full possession. God is for the Thomist "Pure act" meaning that God literally lacks nothing; God is already completely self-sufficient. How such a being could or would ever act in the way we normally understand that term is a mystery within this metaphysical scheme.

or in relation to other beings. There is no "reaching out to another being" that is at the heart of human relationships. But, as we shall argue, relationship and differentiation are essential to agency and agents in relation.

Coreth also wants to retain something of our notion of the person in referring to God. He argues that absolute being is *absolute person*, "for a person, who may be defined as a spiritual subject (*suppositum*), must possess the ontological perfections of the spirit and must be fully autonomous like a single complete substance. But the absolute being is absolute spirit and exists fully, autonomously in itself, as a substance, . . . as a supracategorial one. . . . Absolute being is an individual substance [but] not an individual substance among many others. . . . It is individual only in an analogous sense."[29] And this raises the question of what kind of person God is if God is not a person alongside of or in relationship to other persons. How is a personal relationship with God possible if God is not a person who can relate as one being to another within some kind of common ontological space?

Nevertheless, Coreth claims that "therefore, we must say of God that he is a person, albeit in an analogous sense. He transcends infinitely all the depth and richness of human personality, not by suppressing them, but by 'sublating' [meaning *to negate or eliminate (as an element in a dialectic process) but preserve as a partial element in a synthesis*; this notion is reflective of Hegel's notion of the *aufhebung*] or sublimating them in his own divine personality."[30] But one can ask whether in sublating one person by another the integrity of the two persons as individuals has been retained or whether, in this case, Coreth is subtly moving from radical otherness to undifferentiated oneness in order to preserve the mystery of God, which he locates, in effect, in that which makes God radically different from the limitations of human personality.

At the very end, Coreth says, "God is a *free personal God*. Hence he may speak to us and our question to him might receive an answer, through God's own revelation."[31] Although this seems to be a hopeful note, Coreth has not prepared any basis for thinking, except by a very strained and unpersuasive analogy, that God is free, personal, or capable of speaking or revealing anything, all of which are actions that are performed by an agent. And agents and their agency require a common ontological ground with the other beings toward which their agency is directed. And this ground Coreth has not given us.

---

29. Ibid., 188.
30. Ibid. Material in brackets added by the author.
31. Ibid., 196.

ZimZum

A slightly different take on the same theme can be found in one branch of Jewish mysticism that echoes some of the themes found in Coreth. In Kabbalah, which is gaining popularity among many religious aficionados, a notion known as ZimZum, developed by the medieval rabbinic scholar Isaac Luria, argues that God (En-Sof) is so unlimited that God must restrict Godself in order to enable the created universe to exist at all.[32] God, in other words, could not co-exist with anything other than Godself, given God's absolute otherness, unless God "contracted" Godself so as to make possible the existence of something beside Godself. "The creation has been put by the Absolute outside Itself, and for the appearance of this 'outside' the Absolute had to limit Itself, had to create borders for Its own borderless nature."[33] This is another way that the absolute otherness of God has to be qualified in some way in order for non-divine others to co-exist with (or in) God.

Interestingly, contemporary theologian Jürgen Moltmann has employed the notion of ZimZum in developing his concept of God as Creator out of nothing, *ex nihilo*. Moltmann argues that "in order to create a world 'outside' himself, the infinite God must have made room beforehand for a finitude in himself. It is only by a withdrawal by God into Godself that can free the space into which God can act creatively. The *nihil* for his *creation ex nihilo* only comes into being because—and in as far as—the omnipotent and omnipresent God withdraws his presence and restricts his power."[34] While Moltmann does not specifically articulate the point, I think one might suggest that the notion of the ZimZum withdrawal of God into Godself in order to create a world "outside" of God is an implicit recognition of the need for there to be "room" for God's actions upon and in relation to "others" who are not Godself. If reality is nothing but (or other than) God, then no action is possible since action assumes agent-beings in relation to each other. Moltmann gives God "room" to act only by a divine self-shrinkage or self-contraction. A more basic notion of agency, however, could begin with God as agent standing primordially in relation to other beings, not by an act of self-contraction but by an act of creation. Moltmann's starting point looks suspiciously like a primordial pantheism or panentheism out of which God has to differentiate Godself but precedes the reality of God as Agent.

---

32. See Evgueni Tortchinov, "Studies in Sabbatian Kaballah: Isaac Luria's 'ZimZum'" http://www.kheper.net/topics/Kabbalah/Tzimtzum-ET.htm.

33. Tortchinov, ""Studies in Sabbatian Kaballah."

34. Jürgen Moltmann, *God in Creation* (San Francisco: Harper & Row, 1985), 86–87. See also Moltmann's *The Trinity and the Kingdom* (San Francisco: Harper & Row, 1981), 108–111.

Divine otherness, while ostensibly honoring the difference between God and us, becomes inexplicable when carried too far. John Caputo, a contemporary philosopher, has pointed out that "to say that God or any other thing is wholly other is, *stricto sensu*, impossible. To say the least, God would then be wholly other than whatever is being said by saying that God is wholly other, wholly other even than God, or than God's Godhead, or than the Godhead beyond the Godhead, ad infinitum, no matter to what higher coefficient this negativity is carried."[35] Caputo argues that the logic of radical otherness is that "we will not know whether *wholly other* is a predicate of some being, however exalted, or itself a subject, or a quasi-subject, some kind of dark halo of indeterminancy and anonymity that surrounds and eventually seeps into—and saturates—our lives."[36]

The problem with otherness is that it cannot be articulated without cancelling out the distinction between what is other to the other unless one wants to retreat into meaningless babble, no matter how decked out it is in philosophical terminology.

Paul Tillich

Slightly more comprehensible is the work of Paul Tillich who also argued for the otherness of God as that which is beyond the differentiation of beings with and to each other in the realm of finitude. Tillich argued that God certainly cannot be "a" being—a singular, distinct, individual entity among other entities. If God is to account for the being of other beings beside Godself, God cannot be one being among those beings for whose being God is called upon to account. God must be Being-Itself. God cannot even be the highest being.[37] "If God is *a* being, he is subject to the categories of finitude, especially to space and substance." Any superlatives drawn from finitude (the "highest," most perfect being) become "diminutives. "They place [God] on the level of other beings while elevating him above all of them. . . [But] whenever infinite or unconditional power and meaning are attributed to the highest being, it has ceased to be *a* being and has become being-itself. . . . or as the ground of being."[38] Tillich assumes that all beings must possess the "power of being" if they are to exist and go on existing. But no individual being can provide

---

35. John Caputo, "God is Wholly Other—Almost: '*Différance*' and the Hyperbolic Alterity of God," in *The Otherness of God*, ed. Orrin Summerell (Charlottesville, VA: University Press of Virginia, 1998), 191.
36. Ibid.
37. Paul Tillich, *Systematic Theology*, vol. 1 (Chicago: University of Chicago Press, 1951), 253.
38. Ibid.

the power of being either to itself or to all other beings. The power to be must derive from being-itself, not from an individual being. Being-itself "is beyond finitude and infinity, [it] infinitely transcends every finite being. There is no proportion or gradation between the finite and the infinite. There is no absolute break, an infinite 'jump.' On the other hand, everything finite *participates* in being-itself and in its infinity."[39] Here Tillich is trying to hold in tension both God's utter transcendence ("beyond finitude") and the relation between what God transcends (the finite) and God's reality as Infinitude. For Tillich, relationality is captured in the notion of participation. All finite beings *participate* in the power of being (God) without which they would not *be* at all. The mystery of God is preserved by God's utter transcendence of finitude and God's relationality is preserved by God's being the power of being in which all beings must participate in order to be at all. But participating *in* something is not the same thing as having a relationship *with* that something, especially if that something is a Someone who exists *in relation to* something that is not itself.

Tillich reminds us that every theologian feels compelled to assert both the utter difference between God and what is not God[40] and, at the same time, to assert that God and what is not God are deeply bound together insofar because finite beings need the power of being-itself to be at all. Participation is not, strictly speaking, a relationship *between* beings since God is not a being. Only ontologically distinct beings relate: relation presupposes at least two distinct beings sharing a common ontological ground. But while not relating to beings, God is that in which beings participate or inhere because without that participation that they would not possess the power of being which enables them to be. The notion of participation avoids the problem of God "relating" to another, implying difference and distinction. But participation in God runs the risk of denying the difference between God and what is not God.

One problem faced by those adopting the ontologically transcendent approach to naming God as "Other" is how to explain why a totally self-sufficient, transcendent, wholly Other being would bring into existence something not Godself, something both radically non-divine and a limited other ("the finite"). A traditional answer is "love": God, it is often claimed, wanted to disperse God's greatness out of a superabundance of love for what is not the divine self. God is so great and so saturated with Being that God overspills the divine self into what is not the divine self. But this suggests that

---

39. Ibid., 237. Emphasis added.
40. I am not making any reference to Karl Barth at this point because I want to take up his work in a later chapter on systematic theology's attempt to deal with the problems of God as other and as relational.

there is something missing in God's complete self-sufficiency. While God may not "need" to love, loving fulfills God in a way that not loving cannot. If God is not in any way affected by God's "act" of love, then what kind of love is this? Certainly not a relational kind of love! And if God loves, God can only do so by creating that which is other than Godself. (Unless, of course, what comes from God by emanation, not creation, is not other than God, but is God "dispersed" or temporarily differentiated, as it were.) But this still begs the question: why does something other than God emerge from God if God is absolutely self-sufficient, including, one assumes, the sufficiency of love unless there is something lacking in God's love such that it needs an other in order to fulfill itself? (The doctrine of the Trinity tries to answer this question by pointing to the mutual love of the three persons in the Trinity and we will examine the use of the Trinity in a later chapter. But love, as we finite beings understand it, is always between at least two non-identical persons, implying a distinction between them.)

The Postmodern Critique

But the otherness of God, according to some theologians, can also create an opening for the person seeking a relationship with God. Mark C. Taylor points out that in claiming that we only know what God is *not* then we have, in effect, a knowledge of God. "*[D]ifference from* other is at the same time *relation to other*. Since all things are radically related, everything is thoroughly relative. . . . [This is] the coimplication of everything."[41] Even to claim that God is identical with Godseslf is itself a difference between God and what is not God. In language similar to Coreth's, Taylor says that "difference in itself is self-related difference; as such it is the negativity of itself, the difference not of an other, but *of itself from itself*; it is not itself but its other. But that which is different from difference is identity. Difference is, therefore, itself and identity."[42] Difference and identity are mirror images and suggest, once again, the symbiotic relationship between radical otherness and undifferentiated unity.

The desire for a God who is *not* the object of what is often referred to as the onto-theological approach is found, albeit somewhat obscurely, in the work of a number of postmodern or deconstructionist thinkers. The onto-theological concept of God is one in which God is posited as a transcendent being "outside" or above the ontological conditions of finitude but whose existence can by

---

41. Mark C. Taylor, *Erring: A Postmodern A/Theology* (Chicago: University of Chicago Press, 1984), 108.

42. Ibid., 109.

known through concepts alone, such as in Anselm's ontological argument for the existence of God. The problem with the onto-theological approach to God is that God's radical "otherness" or "alterity" is compromised by being brought within the limits of human conceptuality, which is always "contaminated" or conditioned by the very finitude God is supposed to transcend. The postmodern critics of onto-theology are driven by a fear of categorizing, limiting, defining, or reducing God to the dimensions of human thought, even though that tries to find a ground for the totality of being outside of or beyond finite being, a totality of being that is, in many respects, accessible to the human intellect. The language of being is, after all, human language and when God makes God's own self available to human language, God's divinity is thereby compromised and distorted, or so it is claimed by those who would distinguish God from human beings by an infinite ontological difference. Even the most abstract, deep metaphysical language of being is seen as too restrictive of God, even God as the ground of being. For Jean-Luc Marion, "the transcendence of onto-theology becomes the condition for going beyond the naming, in philosophy, of 'God' as the effective ground"[43] of being.

For example, in his article "God without Being," Marion insists that God is not to be proved rationally or comprehended conceptually.[44] Placing the concept of God within the comprehensive concept of being involves a misguided attempt to determine and comprehend God according to the measure of human concepts.[45]

For Marion, according to Thomas A. Carlson, "by showing too much (a God made present in the presence of a thinking that comprehends), the concepts produced by metaphysics show too little, inasmuch as God by definition exceeds all definition, or inasmuch as God's fullest presence is given to human thought only as absence. The modern destruction of these concepts, therefore, which can leave an apparent void, in fact opens anew a space for thinking and speaking the incomprehensible and ineffable love of the Father."[46]

In traditional metaphysics, something *is* if and only if it is present or presentable to another: objects are construed as beings present to us. This is the metaphysics of presence that posits an identity of being and meaning in which meaning is derived from the presence of being. But what is affirmed

---

43. Jean-Luc Marion, "Metaphysics and Phenomenology: A Summary for Theologians," in *The Postmodern God: A Theological Reader*, ed. Graham Ward (Malden, MA: Blackwell, 1998), 284.

44. See Thomas A. Carlson, "Postmetaphysical Theology," in *The Cambridge Companion to Postmodern Theology*, ed. Kevin Vanhoozer (Cambridge: Cambridge University Press, 2003), 59.

45. Ibid.

46. Ibid., 62–63.

in deconstruction is the *non-coincidence* of being and meaning, what Jacques Derrida calls *différance*. Since God is "the name and the element of that which makes possible an absolutely pure and absolutely self-present self-knowledge," any God talk, any theology, would be thoroughly shaken by *différance* that "blocks every relationship to theology."[47] This creates, at best, a "theology of absence—where the name is given as having no name, as not giving the essence, and having nothing but this absence to make manifest..."[48] According to Derrida, God's "sheer transcendence makes the task of negative theology interminable. By contrast, *différance* is transcendental, not transcendent; it concerns conditions of possibility and impossibility, not eminent or hyper-eminent modes of being. In a sense, both God and *différance* precede Creation; but whereas God was always present to Himself, *différance* 'was' neither a being nor self-present."[49] *Différance* is not a divine being, but it is the condition for thinking God.

This has serious implications for any attempt to speak of God as a personal agent. Emmanuel Levinas has said that our task "will have to be to cancel or exclude the sense of being as an entity, and even of an act of Being, from the language about God."[50] In other words, God is beyond being. In language that seems to echo that of absolute difference and radical transcendence, Levinas says that "God is not simply the 'first other,' the 'other par excellence,' or the 'absolutely other,' but other than the other (*autre qu'autrui*), other otherwise, other with an alterity prior to the alterity of the other . . . transcendent to the point of absence."[51] God is "the Infinite beyond being" and "the transcendence of God cannot be stated or conceived in terms of being."[52] Derrida says that every predication of God must be crossed out in order to glimpse the "*unknowable divinity beyond being*."[53] According to Derrida, "God is above Being"; God is "a Non-God, a Non-Intellect, a Non-Person, a Non-Image . . . He is a pure, clear, limpid one, separated from all duality."[54]

For Marion, who goes further than other postmodern thinkers in the direction of affirming something of God, God is the given (and giver) par

---

47. Kevin Hart, "Jacques Derrida (b. 1930): Introduction," in *The Postmodern God*, 161.
48. Carlson, "Postmetaphysical Theology," 69.
49. Hart, "Jacques Derrida," 163.
50. Robert Gibbs, "Emmanuel Levinas (1906–1995): Introduction," in *The Postmodern God*, 48.
51. Emmanuel Levinas, "God and Philosophy," in *The Postmodern God*, 64.
52. Ibid., 64, 70.
53. Kevin Hart, "Introduction," Jacques Derrida, "From *How to Avoid Speaking*," in *The Postmodern God*, 163. Emphasis added.
54. Ibid., 177.

excellence: God given without restriction, without reservation, without restraint. God gives Godself absolutely. Is Marion suggesting that this is a primordial *action* by God, since giving is an action? And it's not clear to whom or what the giving is made but God seems to be both giver and given simultaneously. "The donation *par excellence* implies an ecstasy outside itself. . . . . the donation that 'God' achieves cannot remain equal to itself (donation as action) except by becoming ecstatic in that which it gives (donation as gift) . . . . the 'God' of phenomenology . . . . acts only to the extent that he does not remain (in) himself."[55]

Marion goes on, "this donation *par excellence* carries with it another consequence: the absolute mode of the presence which saturates each and every horizon, with a dazzling obviousness. Now such a presence without limit (without horizon), which alone precisely matches the donation without reserve, cannot present itself as an object, which of necessity has limits. . . . 'God' in his very dazzlingness shines by his absence. . . . If we saw him, as we see a worldly being, then we would already have ceased to be dealing with 'God.'"[56]

Some postmodern thinkers, such as Michel de Certeau, go so far as to annihilate God's "alterity" (or otherness) as a misleading duality or opposition. He says in the words of Frederick Christian Bauerschmidt, that "same and other become impossible categories in the 'white eschatology' depicted here: *neither* the same, *nor* the other. 'That which *is* without us' is not only beyond the name 'God,' but beyond even the category of 'other.'"[57] When God cannot even be a *personal Other*, then all hope for a meaningful concept of God as personal agent is lost.

Nevertheless, Marion's language tantalizingly, if not dazzlingly, seems not to be able to avoid agent reference because "giving" and "gift" suggests action (God's giving or donation "outside" Godself) even though Marion would resist thinking of God as a primordial agent since agency and agent are categories appropriate to a metaphysics of presence in a common field of being in which objects and subjects encounter each other through reciprocal actions, a field from which God is excluded as an interactive agent. But God's donation "cannot present itself as an object, which of necessity has limits."[58]

I think, in the end, this postmodern or deconstructionist view of God wants to have its cake and eat it too. It wants *something* of God as the "presence

---

55. Marion, "Metaphysics and Phenomenology," 292.
56. Ibid.
57. Frederick Christian Bauerschmidt, "Michel de Certeau (1925–1986): Introduction," in *The Postmodern God*, 140.
58. Marion, "Metaphysics and Phenomenology," 292.

without limit," as an "alterity," an "other," but it does not want to conceptualize this presence in the traditional language of subject-object erected within a common field of being. In its desire not to limit or confine God, even within the categories of Being-Itself, postmodern theology (if that is not a contradiction in terms) abandons all metaphysical categories and ends up merely pointing without words (or with words that only obfuscate or engage in endless play) beyond Being but without abandoning entirely something that "is" beyond Being and therefore "is" the ultimate Reality.

I think the notions of "otherness" and "difference" (spelled with an *e*) can be given a far more relevant and comprehensible meaning in a metaphysics of agency, in which the agents remain both linked and distinct. Postmodernism stresses the delinking of God from every other Being and from Being-Itself in such a way that only the distinctness between God and everything else is retained. That is too high a price to pay for a God who is for us by being in loving relationship with us.

Nishida Kitaro

A similar approach that moves us toward a fuller development of this symbiotic relation between monism and dualism is the work of the contemporary Japanese philosopher Nishida Kitarō who elaborates the notion of identity in and through difference through his concept of *basho*, which means "that which is neither predicated of, nor present in, a subject, nor even the grammatical subject, but that which grounds both, and out of which both arise as specifications or determinations." Basho is "the given-in-intuition prior to the analysis and expression of objectification," the "contradictory self-identity of things." Basho is the final enveloping field about which nothing can be said. It is the basho of absolute nothingness. [59] Technically speaking, basho is a no-self, out of which and on which all distinctions are based. It is an experience "in which no conceptual distinctions are made [and] which allows of no conceptualization, and to which logic applies not at all, or only with contradictory results."[60] Basho is so basic that as an experience it is undifferentiated and beyond all distinctions, including monism and dualism suggesting again that dualism and monism are not radically, in the end, all that different from each other.[61] Nashida seems to be trying to articulate both a

---

59. Robert E. Carter, *The Nothingness Beyond God: An Introduction to the Philosophy of Nishida Kitarō* (New York: Paragon House, 1989), 32, 45.

60. Ibid., 45.

61. Ibid., 14.

radical dualism and a radical oneness, but the paucity of language makes this almost impossible.

The word *nothingness* comes as close as any word to referring to God precisely because it is void of any content that is always reflective of differentiation. "Nothingness, or the formless, is non-dualistic because it is *prior* to any dualism. Nothingness is the non-dualistic whole which is as it is, and before it is sliced up by the dualistic logic of being and non-being."[62]

Nashida admits that "in the purest sense, one cannot speak of absolute nothingness because it is beneath or beyond all distinctions, conceptual categories, or any other means of differentiation . . . because the experience is of an undifferentiated *unity*, and not of Zen's 'forms of the formless.' All *multiplicity* has been eliminated, and both language and logic presuppose there being a differentiated manifold whose essential and accidental structures can be discerned and articulated."[63] Nashida, therefore, does not presuppose that nothingness is an undifferentiated unity, or that the mystical experience is an experience at all. It is the emptiness in which all particular occurrences are to be found.[64]

Echoing the theme of Coreth in seeking God as the presupposition or horizon of ordinary reality, especially rational thinking, Nashida says that the deep self is somehow known "as that at the background of our experience. It is never known but is ever present as a background 'lining' of everything known and knowable."[65] This deeper underlying and grounding is basho. And it is nothingness that is "the enveloper of all things, is the unifier of opposites, the identity of its own self-contradictory expressions."[66] This means that in nothingness or basho we have (to echo Mark Taylor and the philosophy of difference) an *identity of contradictions*, or an *identity of self-contradiction*.

So where does this leave the religious aspirant? Ultimately, Nashida suggests the religious experience is not thought but feeling in and of itself (not a feeling "of" anything). Contentless feeling, he says, is what is left when we imaginatively remove all content from consciousness: there is just formless *awareness*. However, "the nothingness of pure experience, i.e., the self as pure awareness" is not an awareness *of* something external to the awareness.[67]

---

62. Ibid., 83. This reference to nothingness should remind us of John Scotus Erigena whose work was referred to earlier.
63. Ibid., 47–48.
64. Ibid., 48.
65. Ibid., 53.
66. Ibid., 69.
67. Ibid., 85.

Religious experience arises when one becomes aware of a "profound existential contradiction in the depth of his own self" and seeks resolution in contradiction and nothingness. This means letting go of self (as distinct and different) and accepting that I am as an individual an expression of the absolute that is nothing, not something, let alone Someone. I am the absolute's self-negation of itself. The absolute relates itself to itself in the form of self-contradiction. We are at our bottomless depth, empty—literally nothing.[68]

In a way that anticipates our reading of Meister Eckhart, Nashida seems to presuppose a distinction (not, of course, in reality but conceptually) between "God" (as an object of belief and presumably relationship) and God as pure nothingness. It is God as nothingness that is both immanent and transcendent and at most neither because it is beyond (or different from) these categories. "This 'undivided something' out of which even God arises is the nothingness beyond God, which is the ground of God, being, and non-being. It is the ultimate ground of everything."[69]

In a summary set of comments Nashida says, "God is, in the form of nothingness, the pure experience of the formless and undifferentiated *whole* from which, or on which, the ripples and waves of the temporary and differentiated are registered." And "Nothingness is God's face, your face, and my face before any of us were born—that is, before we were individuated." God is absolutely self-contradictory. God is one, and yet God "returns to itself in the form of the infinite many."[70]

One can be excused in thinking that this language borders on the totally obscure and is so different from ordinary language as to be meaningless. But it is, perhaps, this very meaninglessness and paradoxicality in articulating something about God that attracts our deepest religious yearnings. If one is fearful of bringing God "down" conceptually into the muck of finitude by the limitations of ordinary language and thought, then clearly the absolute mystery of God is best preserved by an appeal to literal *non*-sense, to self-contradiction, to nothingness, to the height of paradox and self-contradiction because they reveal the ultimate inadequacy of thought and speech. The question is whether this *kind* of mystery is the kind that religious persons intend when they seek a God who is worthy of their worship and who urges them into relationship with God. (Even to try to articulate the kind of mystery God is uses the language of metaphysics to at least partially demystify God, and thus defeat the purpose of articulation.) I think there is a genuine allure in this mystification of language

---

68. Ibid., 94–95.
69. Ibid., 85–86.
70. Ibid., 87, 89, 96.

about God, but I also think the price we pay for succumbing to the allure is too high precisely because it renders completely problematic any understanding of God as a Someone who can be in relationship with us—not as modes of Godself but as genuine, authentic ontologically real, and distinct "other" beings whose otherness does not compromise our grounding in God's love and power.

G.W.F. Hegel

Nevertheless, the attempt to bring together both difference and identity in a conception of God does capture an insight that one can find somewhat more clearly expressed in the great German philosopher of the nineteenth century G.W.F Hegel.[71] Hegel added a note of dynamic becoming to traditional, more static views of God. God (which for him was Absolute Mind or Thought) could only *become* fully God by going out of Godself and returning to Godself in such a way that the initial otherness between God and what is not God is overcome. This overcoming, however, is a process: it is not static or abstract, since only through a process can the two sides of the dilemma—God as radically Other and God as undifferentiated unity—be brought together. Hegel says in his Introduction to *Hegel's Lectures on the History of Philosophy* that "the development of mind lies in the fact that its going forth and separation constitutes its coming to itself. This being-at-home-with-self or coming-to-self of mind may be described as its complete and highest end: it is this alone that it desires and nothing else. Everything that from eternity has happened in heaven and earth—the life of God, and all the deeds of time—simply are the struggles for mind to know itself, to make itself objective to itself, to find itself, be for itself, and finally unite itself to itself: It is alienated [i.e., made other than itself] and divided, but only so as to be able thus to find itself and return to itself."[72]

And Hegel insists that this self-referential, self-initiated, and self-directed movement of Mind (God) is the only way for God to attain total freedom, for only that reality is free "which is not referred to or dependent on another. True self-possession and satisfaction are only to be found in this, and in nothing else but thought does mind attain this freedom. . . . It is in thought alone that all foreign matter disappears from view and that mind is absolutely free."[73] The "real" God is absolutely self-sufficient and therefore at one with Godself, but

---

71. Carter insists that what Nashida attempts is not a Hegelian synthesis, which resolves thesis and antithesis in an *aufhebung* or sublation, but rather an identity that embraces and preserves thesis and antithesis without any possibility of synthesis. The self is such an identity.

72. G.W.F. Hegel, *On Art, Religion, Philosophy: Introductory Lectures to the Realm of Absolute Spirit*, ed. J. Glenn Gray (New York: Harper & Row, 1970), 230–31.

73. Ibid.

goes out of the divine self only in order to come to know the divine self as the one (and only) reality. All apparently "different" entities are ultimately taken up into God so that God becomes one with Godself and returns to Godself. This "taking up" is part of Hegel's famous notion of the *aufhebung*, which in German means abrogating, annulling, or doing away with, but at the same time preserving at a higher level.[74]

But note that God's return to Godself is not a relational act: God's fulfillment does not come in *relating* to something other. God's own reality is self-identical and self-relating, only passing over into otherness temporarily so as to be able to return to complete self-identity. A view of God who stands in relation to something other than the divine self (through love, for example) is not truly reflective of the Hegelian God. Otherness is, in Hegel's view, an expedient (in a metaphysical and historical process) for God to come to appreciate God's being at home with God's own self (no hospitality for the other here). There is only a slight difference, if any, as we shall see between Hegel's and Eckhart's or Nashida's notions of undifferentiated unity. What difference does exist between their views and Hegel's is that for Hegel it is necessary to *pass through* differentiation (even though it is not ultimately "real" and will be *aufgehoben*) in order to for God to attain non-differentiation. Note also that for Hegel otherness can only be truly overcome by thought since thought can grasp the *concept* of the other and make it its own internally through a mental act, whereas in the external world the other has a bodily, material, factual "otherness" that cannot be overcome (even the notion of overcoming implies resistance to otherness) by thought that is non-material. In the external world, persons meet each other as fully embodied beings that possess both material and non-material dimensions and their relationships cannot be reduced to ones of mutual contemplation or conceptualization without eliminating that which constitutes their fullness as persons.

Ontological Monism and Mysticism

Let us now turn to the fullness of the mystical or ontological monist approach to understanding God. As we explored the various ways in which we struggle to articulate God's difference from everything that is not God, we sensed that the arguments swung back and forth between absolute "otherness" and absolute "oneness." Ontological dualism and ontological monism are symbiotically united twins who, while apparently "different" on the surface, are underneath ultimately reducible to each other. The otherness is stressed when one wants to

---

74. Ibid., 181.

keep God from falling prey to our finite cognition and ontological conditions (dreaded anthropomorphism) and the oneness is stressed when one wants to retain God without having God disappear completely in the beyond or radical otherness and difference that is utter transcendence. But ontological dualism and ontological monism are parasitic on each other, oscillating from one extreme to the other, all in the hopes of rendering God utterly mysterious (so beyond the distinctions of language and thought) while retaining the aura of absolute worshipfulness, which it is assumes depends on God's absolute mystery. Why we want to worship that which is radically unknowable and total mystery is a question that might, perhaps, be best left for the psychologist, not the philosopher or theologian. However that might be, the question, from the side of agency, is whether the religious person can truly worship that which he does not know or relate to as one being to another given that they have no ontological conditions in common.

The driving force behind the mystical (a more common word for negative) approach to God is the desire for the most intimate kind of contact or relationship with the absolute mystery that God "is." But what is so problematic about emphasizing the utter mystery of God is that God either becomes absolutely "other" (and thus unknowable and non-relational) or God becomes the totality of all things, rendered "available" to us in a final spasm of the absolute oneness and identity of all things with each other so that even their otherness is swallowed up in oneness or unity without distinctions. It is this latter consequence that characterizes radical forms of mysticism. (I do not include in this understanding of mysticism a more popular form of it: the desire for a personal union with something that still remains, even after the union has been consummated, other or different from the one seeking the union. The philosophies of mysticism are replete with debate on just what constitutes the union between self and God and whether the self disappears "into" God or somehow retains its individuality or otherness even while being intimately "in" God. The more common form of mysticism rarely goes as far as the annihilation of the self in the union.)

As we have seen earlier, an anthropomorphic conception "pictures" or "figures" God as a person, a being with personal characteristics such as consciousness, will, intention, and the power to act upon God's intentions and, by acting, effect changes in the world. This anthropomorphic picture of God draws from our experience of ourselves as finite, embodied, intentional, conscious, and relational agents, who then apply the personal characteristics drawn from this experience to a being greater than ourselves. But anthropomorphism assumes (rather naively, argue classical and negative theology) that the greatness of God is merely a matter of degree, not of ontology. Anthropomorphism may extol God as stronger, wiser, more knowledgeable, and more compassionate than other beings that inhabit a common ontological space with God, but it cannot cut the cord that binds God to that space. There has to be such a common ontological space if God is even to be compared with them since comparison assumes some common ground on the basis of which the comparison is to be made. God in the anthropomorphic view is one being among many others, distinguished from them by comparative degrees of greatness and not by incommensurate or ontological difference.

A mystical or monist view of God repudiates this kind of anthropomorphism as a religiously fatal reduction or diminution of God to the merely human level, making God accessible to our limited, finite, creaturely, and even sinful and distorted imagination and mentality. It thereby implicates God in a common ontological space that makes it impossible for God to be its creator and sustainer (since God would not be absolutely "beyond" or transcendent of it). Religiously speaking, this kind of God seems to shrivel the religious aspiration to something horribly mundane, limited, and unworthy of that which deserves our worship. In classical theology, the worship of beings like ourselves, even those that are incredibly greater than we are, is the very meaning of idolatry. On this basis, then, no conception of God as a personal agent in any straightforward or direct sense can even get started.

Meister Eckhart

Louis Dupre said that "the mystical drive to live in the experienced presence of God (in whatever degree) belongs to the core of all religion. Without this living flame to warm its life, religion rapidly degenerates into moralism, ritualism, legalism, or pure speculation."[75] I want now to pursue the logic of mysticism in the form of ontological monism or undifferentiated oneness. I do so in part in the spirit of Johann Wolfgang von Goethe who is reported to have said, "In old age we all become mystics."[76] What exactly mysticism is, and how it manifests itself across a variety of different religions, is an enormous and complex issue. I want to focus my reflections on the logic of mysticism on two influential (if not completely representative) attempts to articulate the notion of mysticism.

---

75. Louis Dupré, "*Unio mystica:* The State and the Experience," in *Mystical Experience and Monotheistic Faith: An Ecumenical Dialogue*, ed. Moshe Idel and Bernard McGinn (New York: Macmillan, 1989), 7.

76. Louis Dupré, *Religion and the Rise of Modern Culture* (Notre Dame, IN: University of Notre Dame Press, 2008), 64.

One will be from the medieval Christian mystic Meister Eckhart and the second from a contemporary philosopher, W.T. Stace.

Meister Eckhart, the late thirteenth-century Christian theologian and mystic, captures brilliantly and expresses eloquently the aspiration among many Christians to find and articulate the deepest possible unity with God, to overcome what is often characterized as the alienating difference or otherness between God and them. In fact, Eckhart went so far as to court heresy, a heresy that grew directly out of his attempt to close the gap between God and what is ostensibly other than God. His heresy threatened to annihilate any ontological difference between God and us, a difference that the Church was committed to preserving (primarily through ontological dualism) even when it could only do so at the cost of logical consistency given its assumption that nothing could be truly "other" than God standing over against us. In Eckhart, we will continue to see how non-differentiation (monism) and radical otherness (dualism) keep playing off against each other and ultimately coming into co-implication so that one always leads to the other and back again, and finally settling down into the triumph of monism.

At the heart of Eckhart's work are the convictions that "every distinction is foreign to God" and that there is a fundamental, ontological difference (I know that sounds paradoxical) between thinking of *God* as a being standing in relation to us and thinking or aspiring to the *Godhead*, which is, for Eckhart, the "real" God, who is beyond relationality, difference, and distinction. In writing of the Godhead as undifferentiated unity, Eckhart, like any rational person, is condemned to use language that is inherently shot through with the characteristics of differentiation. Language draws distinctions in order to communicate meaning and reference. One cannot refer to anything without distinguishing that thing from other things. The very subject/predicate form of language rests on the primordiality of differentiation. Language will speak "of" God as an object: to use object-laden language to deny that God is an object is virtually impossible because one must refer to the object that one is claiming is not an object because it is non-differentiated and reference implies differentiation. Thus to use language to express non-differentiation is inherently problematic, even paradoxical, and the best writers of mystical oneness will acknowledge that fact. (Aquinas is reputed to have had a mystical experience after which he wrote nothing more and declared that all that he had written was, in comparison to the mystical experience granted to him, worth nothing more than straw.)

Let's unpack Eckhart's basic convictions and explore their implications for his understanding of God. There is no doubt that his attempt to put into metaphysical discourse a deeply felt religious/spiritual dimension of God's being indicates that he is trying to reconcile the relational strain with the monist and dualist strains in religious experience. The reference to distinctions being foreign to God is actually taken not directly from Eckhart but rather is found in Pope John XXII's Bull directed against his work.[77] Eckhart is accused by the Pope of wishing to know more than he should and of presenting "many things as dogma that were designed to cloud the true faith in the hearts of many."[78] It is not clear whether Eckhart is being quoted directly, but the Pope asserts that "as is evident from [his] confession" he "preached, taught and wrote twenty-six articles," one of which refers to distinctions being foreign to God. While this particular assertion is not declared heretical it is deemed by the Pope to be "quite evil-sounding and very rash and suspect of heresy, though with many explanations and additions that might take on or possess a Catholic meaning."[79]

It may be possible, of course, that Eckhart engaged in what to a purely rational mind seem strange and outlandish paradoxical statements about God precisely in order to deconstruct or problematize the categories of reason and logic so that God can break through them into the individual in a way that goes beyond the restrictions of logic. If, as Eckhart insists, it is only a malign intention that could make him a heretic, then language that seems on the surface to undermine the traditional language about God enshrined in the liturgies and creeds of the Church could well have been intended to deepen his hearer's faith, pushing it below (or above) the literal meaning of the words he uttered. We find in Eckhart, as Edmund Colledge and Bernard McGinn say, the "absolute centrality of apophaticism" (as first seen in Pseudo-Dionysius. See above).

I do not intend to explore whether Eckhart was truly heretical or whether the evidence cited against him by the Pope is absolutely representative of everything he said. But Pope John XXII makes the point that through appropriate explanations what seems heretical might be made to possess a meaning faithful Catholics could accept. This has been my point all along: there is something in the approach taken by Eckhart that does speak to and represents an important strain in the religious inclination toward God. My argument has been that this mystical strain, when expressed as a metaphysically primordial understanding of God, stands in extreme tension with the relational strain best articulated in the metaphysics of personal agency that insists upon

---

77. "In agro dominico," March 27, 1329 in *Meister Eckhart: The Essential Sermons, Commentaries, Treatises, and Defense*, trans. Edmund Colledge and Bernard McGinn (New York: Paulist, 1981), 79.

78. Ibid., 77.

79. Edmund Colledge and Bernard McGinn, trans., *Meister Eckhart* (New York: Paulist, 1981), 80.

the primordiality of God being both experienced and represented as a personal agent standing in relationship with human beings.

Even if Eckhart did not say in the exact words quoted in the Bull that distinctions are foreign to God, the corpus of his writing is absolutely consistent with that sentiment. It is clear, for example, that he fully embraces Pseudo-Dionysius's and Erigena's notion of *apophasis*: our inability to speak of God as God is. Eckhart asserts that "God is nameless, because no one can say anything or understand anything about him."[80] One reason for Eckhart's embrace of the apophatic approach to knowledge of God is his conviction that God is not "a" being existing in the same ontological space as other beings. In fact, one of Eckhart's strongest claims is that we have to move beyond "God" as *Someone* in relation to us to what he calls the "Godhead" (though in some contexts he continues to use the word "God" to refer to what is beyond "God," something like Tillich's God beyond the God of theism). Only the context makes clear what his real intention is in each instance.

Only because language seems to require it, Eckhart uses causal sounding language (which he immediately retracts) of God's relation to the world, but his real intention is to identify God with the world or rather to deny the separate reality of the world and instead to absorb it into God. He is, in effect, a radical monist who believes in one single reality in which all (apparently separate and distinct beings) exist. But their distinct existence is, ultimately, an illusion. He does not believe in the traditional classical view of ontological dualism that God is the absolute "other" or in God's transcendence "over" a world that is distinct from God. The notion of transcendence "over" is a form of dualism (two distinct realities) and this distinction is the last obstacle to be overcome as one seeks to annul one's distinctness in the illumination that one *is* the one reality. This leaves, of course, no place for a personal God with whom one can establish a relationship (or have it established by the actions of God).

Eckhart observes that in nature (as understood by our inadequate mental faculties) there are producers (causes) and products (effects). Eckhart eschews the causal language of classical theism. In comparison to causal language, he argues,

> it is clear that in the Godhead, since every production or emanation [using the language of the neo-Platonists, not the biblical language of creation] is not directed to what is outside the producer . . . and what is procreated does not have the nature of something made or created and is not an effect. It is also clear that the producer does not

80. Ibid., 206.

have the nature of a creator or a cause, and that what is produced is not outside the producer and is not different from it, but is one with it. . . . Everything that the One produces that is not an effect, or something made on the outside, is necessarily one inasmuch as it remains in the One. . . . not divided from the One, but one with the One, from the One, through the One and in the One.[81]

In using the language of begetting and begotten, Eckhart says that begetter and begotten are "one in reality, but are opposed and distinct by relation, either by a real relation in the Godhead where the relation and the real being are the same thing [thus annulling, I would argue, the very notion of relation itself]."[82]

This is consistent with Eckhart's view that number and division (the chief characteristics of distinct entities) belong to imperfect things, not to the Godhead. Distinction is a departure from the One so that the "fall" is from the One into two and later into the many. And the greater the departure from the One "the more offensive a thing is to God and nature."[83] Multitude or manyness is always a "sin."[84] "God is one in all ways and according to every respect so that he cannot find multiplicity in himself either in intellect or in reality . . . no distinction can exist or be understood in God himself. . . . Every distinction is foreign to God."[85] Distinctions are "lost" in God.

Significantly, the chief culprit for Eckhart in creating departure and distinction is the *act*: "Every act creates a distinction."[86] And that is why the notion of God as an agent is fundamentally inimical to Eckhart's metaphysics of the undifferentiated oneness that is God, and why it will always, on the basis of this metaphysics, be in radical tension with a metaphysics grounded in the primordiality of agents and actions. But clearly the (overt) language of the Bible is the language of divine action, which makes it impossible to reconcile (at least without complex philosophical and theological maneuvering) with Eckhart's brand of mysticism, no matter how compelling his mysticism is to the religious sensibilities attuned to the deepest mystery of God.

Compounding the audacity of what he is saying, Eckhart asserts "something [he has] never said before. When God created the heavens, the earth and creatures, he did not *act*. He had nothing to do. He made no effort."[87]

---

81. Ibid., 96–97.
82. Ibid., 73.
83. Ibid., 99.
84. Ibid., 166.
85. Ibid., 79.
86. Ibid., 161.

Paradoxically deploying the language of difference or differentiation, Eckhart says that in this respect "God and the Godhead are as different from each other as heaven and earth." In the Godhead there is only unity and therefore "nothing to talk about." But "God acts. The Godhead does not. It has nothing to do and there is nothing going on in it. It never is on the lookout for something to do. The difference between God and the Godhead is the difference between action and nonaction."[88]

The God who is referenced in worship as creator is not the Godhead. "For before there were creatures, God was not god, but, rather, he was what he was. When creatures came to be and took on creaturely being, then God was no longer God as he is in himself, but god as he is with creatures."[89] Creation is a falling away from unity and simplicity.[90] It is better to say that God "produces," "begets," or "emanates" the world (rather than to say that God creates it as a cause brings about an effect). But in this "production" God does not produce something "outside" God's own self. "It is clear that in the Godhead, since every production or emanation is not directed to what is outside the producer, and is not from something that is not an existing being or from nothing, and in the third place is not directed to particular existence, what is procreated does not have the nature of something made or created and is not an effect. It is also clear that the producer does not have the nature of a creator or a cause, and that what is produced is not outside the producer and is not different from it, but is one with it."[91] Creation in the biblical sense makes God (not the Godhead) relational, and that is why this God must be annihilated or forsaken. Relationality is simply another way of referring to distinction and is antithetical to the true nature of the Godhead.

The Godhead is not the highest goal of creation. "Therefore, we pray that we may be rid of god, and taking the truth, break into eternity. . ."[92] And when I achieve this breakthrough I will discover "that God and I are one. . . . for I am the unmoved Mover, that moves all things."[93] One of the central charges of heresy against Eckhart is found just here: his claim that in his soul he is one with Christ who is one with God, without distinction. "Wherever

---

87. Raymond B. Blakney, trans., *Meister Eckhart: A Modern Translation* (New York: Harper & Brothers, 1941), 225. Emphasis in original
88. Ibid., 226.
89. Ibid., 228.
90. Colledge and McGinn, *Meister Eckhart*, 91.
91. Ibid., 96.
92. Blakney, *Meister Eckhart*, 229.
93. Ibid., 232.

God is the Father and the unbegotten begetter, there is the begotten Son too. Therefore, since God is in me, surely God the Father begets the Son in me, and in me the begotten Son himself is one and undivided. . ."[94] The point of contact (though ultimately it is not, of course, a contact between distinct beings) is the *vunkelin*, the spark of God in the soul, "so closely akin to God that it is an undivided simple one, and bears within itself the images of all created things, images without images and images beyond images." This language is appropriate because it is trying to refer to that which is not distinct and which cannot be thought discursively or in the ways in which thinking *about* the world and the "other" normally takes place. This spark is an uncreated light that has "never touched either time or place. This spark rejects all created things, and wants nothing but its naked God." It is not content "with the simple divine essence in its repose . . . it wants to go into the simple ground, into the quiet desert, into which distinction never gazed, not the Father, nor the Son, nor the Holy Spirit."[95]

What the spark wants requires that a person, as a distinct individual, must thoroughly annihilate himself so as to prepare himself to have God "pour the whole of himself into this man, or else he is not God . . . God must pour out the whole of himself with all his might so totally into every man who has utterly abandoned himself that God withholds nothing of his being or his nature or his entire divinity . . ."[96] and this means that I and Christ are one since all that is divine is in me and I in it.

This position is necessitated by Eckhart's view that if Christ is "distinct" from me, then Christ has no value for me because distinction is an ontological gap (actually an illusion), and therefore an ontological barrier that even God's grace cannot cross to make me one with God.[97] Even the conception of God *acting* in grace *upon* something other is a profound violation of primordial Eckhartian principles because it presupposes distinctions between God and that upon which God acts and it presupposes divine action (and an agent responsible for it) in a field of action in the first place.

Naturally, all this leads to the incomprehensibility of God by a human intellect that thinks discretely and discursively and presupposes distinctions. These distinctions of thought are as basic as those between the thinker, the thought and its intentional object, and between objects themselves. But knowledge of God requires the transcendence (or absence) of these marks of

94. Ibid., 267.
95. Colledge and McGinn, *Meister Eckhart*, 198.
96. Ibid., 197.
97. Ibid., 167.

human thought. Eckhart believes the only way to even approach a knowledge of God is by turning inward (away from the deceptive multiplicity of the world). This means a simplicity of self, or a self able to see, or as Eckhart audaciously puts it, "the pure, naked divine being without a medium . . . contemplat[ing] God's naked being without distinction."[98] But there is no hint of how to contemplate anything without some distinctions except in the excess of the mystical ecstasy that is beyond thought, language, comprehension, and expression.

One significant consequence of the Eckhartian position (and thereby of ontological monism) is that any notion of the self having a moral will that is distinct from God's will is absolutely negated. Eckhart can talk as if our will must be submitted to God's will but in the end, given his metaphysical presuppositions, those wills cannot ultimately be distinct. Carried to an extreme, this leads Eckhart to assert that if he has sinned it must be because God has "caused" (using the term loosely) him to sin and he must feel no regret for those sins. "Since God in some way wills for me to have sinned, I should not will that I had not committed sins."[99] One corollary of all this is Eckhart's emphasis on "detachment" or "disinterest" toward worldly things (since the alternative is to become tied to what is other than myself, thus perpetuating distinction). The high virtue is "pure disinterest, that is, detachment from creatures" and this is "above love because love compels me to suffer for God's sake, whereas disinterest makes me sensitive only to God."[100] Disinterest "comes so close to zero that nothing but God is rarefied enough to get into it, to enter the disinterested heart."[101] "Unmovable disinterest brings man into his closest resemblance to God. It gives God his status as God. His purity is derived from it, and then his simplicity and unchangeable character."[102] It is clear why this notion of disinterest must trump or even replace love because love is fundamentally relational and attaches two or more beings to each other. Love presumes "otherness" because it is the deepest possible interest by one being *in the other for the sake of the other*. And love is predicated on relationality and the primordiality of action that expresses love. This agential, personal, and relational primordiality is totally antithetical to Eckhart's primordiality of undifferentiated oneness.

---

98. Ibid., 191.
99. Ibid., 79.
100. Blakney, *Meister Eckhart*, 82.
101. Ibid., 83.
102. Ibid., 85.

I believe Eckhart is rigorously consistent in drawing out these implications of his absolute monism or his ideal of undifferentiated oneness. They reflect the metaphysical consequences of starting with the assumption that God cannot be a distinct being whose "otherness" in some way stands in relation to us and other beings. But remember we have only three choices, two of which actually boil down to one. Primordially, there is multiplicity all around: there is one absolute distinction (that between the utterly transcendent otherness of God and everything else); and there is no distinction at all but only undifferentiated oneness. I am arguing that the latter two choices ultimately collapse into one. If one pushes the logic of absolute ontological transcendence far enough, the transcendent "Other" becomes absolutely irrelevant to what is Other than one's "otherness." Total and absolute transcendence cannot be conceptualized, pointed to, articulated, or expressed precisely because it transcends all the categories and terms of articulation and conceptualization. It even runs into a logical conundrum: how one can express radical transcendence unless one has some conception of the nature of the two realities that are in a "relation" of transcended and transcending? Utter transcendence eventually collapses into undifferentiated oneness in order to avoid the problem of having to express a transcendence that is so utterly other that it cannot be brought into a relation with that which it transcends. If one moderates or mitigate the absoluteness of the transcendence without abandoning some sense of distinction then one winds up, I believe, with multiplicity. And it is only in an ontology of multiplicity (of distinct beings) that one can find the appropriate metaphysical context for thinking of God as a personal agent.

W.T. Stace

Building to some extent on the work of Eckhart, contemporary philosopher Walter Stace has argued that mysticism is primarily an *experience*, not a set of concepts or metaphysical ideas reflecting an ontological state. However, the experience does eventually yield concepts that in varying degrees of adequacy attempt to reflect the experience without ever being able to represent it fully and perfectly or stand in complete isomorphic relation to it. All mystical experiences are, according to Stace, essentially "ineffable," that is, incapable by their very nature of being captured or articulated in language (though they may be "expressed" through language and in other ways, which are themselves also essentially experiential—a non-rational, non-cognitive *sense* of ineffable joy, oneness with reality, ecstasy, etc.).

Again, stumbling toward a way of setting forth in words what is itself ineffable, Stace argues that the "core" of mysticism is an "apprehension of *an ultimate nonsensuous unity in all things*, a oneness or a One to which neither the senses nor the reason can penetrate. . . . it entirely transcends our sensory-intellectual consciousness." [103] This unity is *undifferentiated*. Quoting from the Mandukya Upanishad, Stace claims that the core of the mystical experience is an "undifferentiated unity—a oneness or unity in which there is no internal division, no multiplicity."[104] Human sensory-intellectual consciousness refers to the way in which we know empirical, material finite objects in the world around us; they are known by being sensed by us through one or more of our sensory organs: seen, felt, tasted, smelled, or heard. But this way of knowing only yields knowledge (if it can even be called knowledge) of entities that share and exist in the same limitations of the STMW in which we (or at least our bodies) are enmeshed and, some in the Platonic tradition might say, entombed. The mystical experience promises to lift us above, away from, or beyond the limits or fetters of this world and into non-differentiated union with that which utterly transcends it by annulling all differentiation entirely. Transcending the STMW means, for the mystic, eventually overcoming the distinction between the transcendent and that which it transcends since that is still a distinction and can only be overcome by "descending" into the non-sensuous unity of an undifferentiated oneness. As we have suggested, ontological dualism (the transcendent and that which it transcends) leads eventually to ontological monism in which the difference presupposed by transcendence is swamped ontologically by oneness without duality between the transcendent and the transcended.

Stace is careful to point out that one of the most frustrating conditions of the spatio-temporal-material matrix in which we are ensnared is that there is always a difference or a distinction that has to be drawn between one object and another. This matrix is characterized at its deepest level as a "world" of ontologically distinct independent entities or beings, each existing somehow differentiated from the others. As we have seen, the very nature of language (on which sensory-intellectual thought depends to articulate what it "knows") presupposes a multitude of differentiations in the world, not least those that distinguish us (and our consciousness) from that *of which* we are conscious. I cannot speak intelligibly without using a verb, an intentional object, and a predicate: "The cat on the mat is black." This claim about what is the case with

103. Walter T. Stace, *The Teachings of the Mystics* (New York: New American Library, 1960), 14–15.
104. Ibid., 20.

respect to the cat only makes sense if we can differentiate the cat from the mat and from everything else that is not the cat. The cat about which we are attempting to make truth-claims must be distinguishable from the other entities in its field of existence. And our language is structured so as to reflect these distinctions.

There is a philosophical debate about whether, as Kant would argue, I bring to my experience of the world a "transcendent*al*" set of categories (e.g., space, time, number) which I "impose" upon the world and without which I cannot "think" the world. Others argue that my experience of the world precedes these categories and determines which ones are appropriate for representing that world. For my purposes the resolution of this debate is not directly relevant since I simply want to recognize that the language we use to assert what we believe is true of the world presupposes subject-object distinctions and attributes predicates or characterizations to the objects about which I am speaking.

We have now completed our analysis of ontological dualism and ontological monism as two ways of approaching a knowledge and, ultimately, an experience of God. I now want to turn to that external world of embodied relationships to find the primordial concept of personal agency on which to build a notion of God as the chief exemplification of what it means to be a personal agent, an agent whose being is defined, in part, through relationships with other agents created and sustained through personal actions.

2

Establishing the Primordiality of the Agent, Act, and Agency

Let us begin our task of establishing the primordiality of conceiving God through the categories of agent/agency/action by where we start any metaphysical reflection. Let us start with the immediate experience we have of ourselves as agents. If you have been following my presentation so far, you have been actively engaged as an agent. You have *done* or *performed* a whole variety of actions. You have held a book in your hands, you have sent your gaze across a page, you have sat down (and occasionally stood up), you have gone off to get a cup of coffee, and you have focused your thoughts upon the words in front of you. Each of these *doings* is an action, and you are the agent who has performed or done them. There are, of course, many things that have also been going on in you simultaneously which are not, strictly speaking, actions of yours. You have probably not chosen or intended to blink your eyes, or to keep your heart beating, or to maintain a rhythmic breathing, but these things have happened. They have occurred, but you have not consciously intended them to happen and thus they are not, strictly speaking, actions you have performed. Fortunately, we already have a basis for distinguishing between these two different kinds of occurrences: one we call actions (consciously intended by you, the agent) and the other we call events (happenings that occur without any conscious action or intent on your part).

Notice in my previous paragraph that I snuck in, as one action among many, the action of thinking—for that is the key to understanding ourselves primarily as agents rather than as thinkers. If we step back in reflection to think about our fundamental nature as selves, we perform an action. Stepping back into reflection, or engaging in a thought process, is an act of the self—it is something we choose to do. On the other hand, acting is not simply another word for thinking (though acting is often accompanied by thinking). This is the simple basis for claiming that we are primordially agents, one of whose actions is thinking about what it means to be an agent. At one point in the history of philosophy we got sidetracked (e.g., Descartes) into thinking that the primordial nature of the self was as thinker and forgot that thinking is an action. And once we started at that point, we then had to find a way to establish the fact that we were also agents. But from the view that the self is primarily a thinker, it is very difficult to establish the primordiality of action since action is not restricted to thinking, though thinking is an action. We must first be an agent in order to engage in the act of thinking, an act through which we hope to arrive at a fundamental definition of the self. But if we conclude from this intellectual exercise that thinking is the basic characteristic of the self, as did Descartes, our conclusion hides from us the very basis on which our thinking was carried out in the first place: the fact that we engaged, as agents, in an act of thinking in order to reach the absurd conclusion that we are not primarily agents but thinkers. How odd that as agents we use one of the modes of action available to us (thinking) to conclude that we are not primarily agents at all but thinkers whose thinking is divorced from the ground of action from which it proceeds. This is not to say, of course, that thinking is not essential to our fullness as personal agents, but it is only one of the many actions open to us and is embedded in the more basic or primordial characteristic of the self: our capacity for agency.

John Macmurray

The philosopher John Macmurray, in his much underappreciated book *The Self as Agent*, made the significant argument that if we think of ourselves from the standpoint of agency we can establish the primordiality of being agents, one of whose actions is thinking whereas if we think from the standpoint of thinking, we cannot arrive at an understanding of ourselves as agents. It would be ridiculous to say one of our most important thoughts is action since action is not thought but doing. If thinking alone defines the self, then how is action possible? But if action defines the self, then naturally thinking is possible because it is an action of the self. The trick, philosophically, is to think from the standpoint of what is more basic to the self: thinking or action. As Macmurray argues, in thinking we want to eliminate as much as possible any of the non-cognitive dimensions of ourselves (our feelings, mental distractions, bodily sensations, etc.). In other words, we want to segregate our thinking from the inclusive range of things that constitute us as agents engaged in multiple, mostly non-cognitive, ways with the world. "The 'purer' our thought becomes, the more it excludes not merely perception, but all sensuous elements, and moves in a shadowy world of abstract and general ideas."[1] But inclusion is the chief characteristic of action. "Action . . . is a full concrete activity of the self in which all our capacities are employed; while thought is constituted by the exclusion of some of our powers and a withdrawal into an activity which is less concrete and less complete."[2] This leads Macmurray to conclude that "[t]he concept of 'action' is *inclusive*. As an ideal limit of personal being, it is the concept of an unlimited rational being, in which all the capacities of the Self are in full and unrestricted employment." Significantly, he also adds that "as limited and finite persons, such a fullness of positive being lies beyond our range."[3] (This raises the possibility of what I have referred to as a more sophisticated anthropomorphism because it suggests the possibility of a view of God as a fuller, less limited, more inclusive "positive" being, the full extent of whose attributes lies beyond the cognitive and practical range of our capacities, but who is not outside our ontological space entirely.)

Macmurray also suggests that "pure" thought, as an ideal limit, "denotes an activity of the Self which is purely formal and completely without content. Now purely formal thought is equivalent to nothing; for there cannot be a form which is not the form of something, and a purely formal activity is therefore an activity which is no activity. . . . 'Pure thought' is not merely impossible *for us*, it is impossible in the nature of things."[4] I would suggest that the pure thought Macmurray refers to is equivalent to the monistic ontology of undifferentiated oneness, or the dualistic "otherness" to which the dualistic ontology refers. The attempt to preserve God's mystery through the apophatic approach, emptiness, undifferentiated oneness, radical otherness, and nothingness are the result of pushing thought beyond all content. But one can only start down that road once one has abandoned any attempt to think reality through the basic category of agency and action, the very categories that are presupposed by someone starting down any road, either cognitive or practical.

One implication of starting our understanding of the self from the standpoint of action is that we "know" in acting that we are engaged with the "other." The other is the world in which our action takes place. Action is the attempt to modify the world that is both outside us and in which we are simultaneously embedded. The socio-temporal-material world (STMW) is neither alien to us nor are we completely absorbed into or fully identified with it. Each one of us is an agent, an originator of action, whose actions directly affect other agents as well as non-agents in an ontological space that

---

1. John Macmurray, *The Self as Agent* (London: Faber & Faber, 1957), 86.
2. Ibid.
3. Ibid., 87.
4. Ibid., 88.

we jointly occupy with them. We don't need to establish by thought the reality of the world "outside" us because we already "know" its reality through the primordiality of action that we are already part of and engaged in something other than ourselves at a more basic level than thinking. Acting establishes our knowledge of the world. If we try to establish it solely by thinking, we have no way to distinguish between true and illusory views of the world (except, of course, by acting on our ideas to find out which ones enable us to find our way successfully in the world). As Macmurray says, "thinking presupposes knowledge. [But] our knowledge of the world is primarily an aspect of our action in the world. . . . We can only think about what we already know. This primary knowledge is knowledge that arises in action."[5] It is what is often simply called knowledge from experience.

Of course, we often find that what we intend our action to accomplish is frustrated by the often recalcitrant world in which that action is being "inserted" or embedded. For example, imagine I try to slap the wasp that has landed on my wrist. But I miss and the wasp stings me. Clearly the intention guiding my action was not realized. At this point I will be well advised to stop slapping and start thinking about what to do in such cases in the future. Thinking allows me to withdraw temporarily from direct action in order to figure out (and in this way human agents have an advantage over other animals) what other courses of action might to open to them. But whatever I come up with in my reflective withdrawal must ultimately be tested for its appropriateness by being acted upon. In other words, as Macmurray says, "the question which a theoretical activity seeks to answer can only arise in practical experience, directly or indirectly; and the answer can be true or false only through a reference to action. Thought cannot provide a criterion of truth, but at most a criterion of the correctness of the process of thinking."[6]

Of course, one of the most serious objections to conceiving the self as primarily agent comes from contemporary science. Many scientists, especially those committed to a kind of evolutionary epistemology, regard the self as essentially a complex mechanism or biological organism composed of smaller and even more basic parts, none of which are intentional or agential. Human beings, they argue, are not fundamentally or ontologically different from the parts out of which they are composed; they are simply more complex arrangements of those parts. And if those parts are not themselves conscious or

---

5. Ibid., 101.

6. Ibid.,102. Taken simply at face value, of course, this claim is not correct. Pure mathematics, for example, probably does not arise from a problem in practical experience. Nor does this claim resolve the problems (and potentialities) of some kind of pragmatism.

intentional, then the human beings to whom they give rise during the course of evolution are not conscious or intentional. No ontological gap needs to be crossed in the process of evolution from the non-personal, non-agential to the emergent human agent because what has "emerged" is neither personal intentional nor even an agent.[7]

I want to look at the implications of this scientific claim for our understanding of personal agency through two complementary lenses. First, I want to show that it fails to explain our experience of being agents. I will argue that our sense of agency grows out of our direct and practical engagement with the world of the "other." Second, I want to show that as agents, we preside hierarchically over an infrastructure containing sub-acts that, at the appropriate level, can be explained scientifically. But the agent presiding over that infrastructure can be explained by categories appropriate only to agents, not to a non-agential substructure. I will draw upon the work of two major contemporary philosophers, Edward Pols and Raymond Tallis, both of whose work complements that of John Macmurray though neither mentions him at all,. No one, to my knowledge, has brought these thinkers together in a single presentation. And in the case of Pols and Tallis, neither, I suspect, would fully support the view of God that I intend to draw from their work, though I think I can tease out that view without doing violence to their fundamental categories and arguments. Following the establishment of the primordiality and explanatory power of personal agency, I will conclude by examining how to apply this category to divine actions and, in particular, to how divine actions intersect or mesh with human actions and natural events within the STMW without causing conceptual incoherence.

Raymond Tallis

Raymond Tallis is a polymath of the first order. He has been a physician, a professor of geriatric medicine, a gerontologist, a philosopher, and a cultural and literary critic, among many other things. Of particular importance for this study, he is the author of a trilogy on human nature and knowing. The trilogy began with *The Hand: A Philosophical Inquiry Into Human Being*[8] (2003). It was followed by *I Am: A Philosophical Inquiry Into First-Person Being*[9] (2004), and the

---

7. This is not to deny the habit of some scientists, such as Richard Dawkins, to anthropomorphize some of these more basic elements such as genes, which, as he says, "intend" their own survival. The dangers of anthropomorphism run downward as much as upward.

8. Raymond Tallis, *The Hand: A Philosophical Inquiry Into Human Being* (Edinburgh: Edinburgh University Press, 2003).

final volume is *The Knowing Animal: A Philosophical Inquiry Into Knowledge and Truth*[10] (2005).

In *The Hand*, Tallis sets out to explore "the distinctive mystery of human nature," "the ontological distinctness of humans,"[11] or the "exceptional nature" of humans as something not reducible to the categories of human biology or its physical infrastructure. He wants to establish what it means for the human self to have "true agency."[12] In this sense, his project is identical to those of Macmurray, Pols, and me. In Tallis's view, the most important original distinction between the non-human animal and the personal agent is the latter's unique use of its hand. We should note that Tallis's approach closely resembles Macmurray's notion that the fundamental initial contact with the other is not through thought but through physical contact. For Macmurray, the primary sense contact with the world is *touch* or feel. Touch is the experience of the other as other (than me) since it resists the push of the hand or finger and thereby establishes itself as other than myself. It is significant that in the history of philosophy and epistemology it has been sight or vision that has been privileged as the basic sense metaphor for representing thought's connection to the reality beyond the thinker. But sight operates only at a distance [13] and can easily be deceptive. Touch, on the other hand, "involves physical contact between the organ of sense and the object perceived, while vision is incompatible with this. . . . Tactual perception is *necessarily* perception in action. To touch anything is to exert pressure upon it, however slight, and therefore, however slightly, to modify it." The result is, according to Macmurray, that the act of touching is prior to the act of seeing as the basis for knowing the other.[14] (Touch also involves some resistance by the object being touched to the one doing the touching. This resistance is essential to establishing the singular identities of beings independent of but not beyond relationality with the self. The implications of a being having an independent identity and as resistant to some degree to the actions of the other for conceiving God's relation to a world that is not Godself will be spelled out in due course.)

---

9. Raymond Tallis, *I Am: A Philosophical Inquiry Into First-Person Being* (Edinburgh: Edinburgh University Press, 2004).

10. Raymond Tallis, *The Knowing Animal: A Philosophical Inquiry Into Knowledge and Truth* (Edinburgh: Edinburgh University Press, 2005).

11. Tallis, *The Hand*, 8, 13.

12. Ibid., 14.

13. Macmurray, *The Self as Agent*, 107.

14. Ibid.

For Tallis, the primary means we have for touching the other is the human hand. The use of the hand awakens a sense of the user (the self) as an agent with choices as to *how* to use the hand. Because of the versatility of the hand, it can be used for a variety of grips and when the hand-owner becomes aware of this versatility, he or she must make a choice as to which use is most appropriate for achieving the purpose he or she has in mind. And with this choice "comes a consciousness of action: the arbitrariness of choice between two equally sensible ways of achieving the same goal awakens the sense of agency."[15] Tallis contends that the awareness of the hand as a tool to accomplish intentions enabled humans "to pass into the realm of agency [presumably from a stage in which their agency had not yet been fully developed or actualized]."[16] Non-human animals reach for things, but this is not intentional. But, says Tallis, "human fingering and manipulation are 'doing.' Much of what is proximal to the wrist is shared with animals; distal to the wrist we have no peers. *And it is what happens distal to the wrist that, in the first instance, imports true 'doing' into the world.* Agency (and the agentive self) grows from the tips of our 'meta-fingering' fingers. This, then, retroacts upon what is proximal to the wrist, importing doing into more and more of the body, and, via tools, into what happens beyond the wrist, making the world increasingly the product of doing rather than happening."[17] (Happening is occurrence *in* or, to use Macmurray's phrase, modification *of* the world exterior to the self but without the intentionality, consciousness, or volition essential to purposive agentive doing. It is event, not act.) "When we seize hold of things, we select the grips that we deploy. (This reference to deployment of what he will call the "infrastructure" of action will be developed more extensively in my upcoming treatment of the work of Edward Pols who will, in effect, elaborate Tallis's claim that the tool-like status of the hand instrumentalises the human organism and "it is this that ignites the sense of agency."[18]) Although there are constraints on the possible range of actions from which we choose, "these are not so narrow that the grips can be regarded as entirely pre-programmed and/or instinctual; nor so wide that random movements would suffice. In our uniquely human manipulations of the world outside of our bodies, we are truly agents and our hands are the instruments of our agency."[19] In fact, one could argue that the very notion of "tool" implies its conscious use for a particular purpose by a tool-wielder.

15. Tallis, *The Hand*, 175.
16. Ibid., 69.
17. Ibid.
18. Ibid., 295.
19. Ibid., 195.

And in this sense, "tool" implies conscious agency on the part of the tool-user. A rock does not "use" its hard shell as a tool to protect it from hammer blows because it is not a conscious object capable of taking actions to protect itself. To think otherwise would truly be anthropomorphism run amuck in the downward direction. "An object becomes a tool only when it is linked to an agent, to a subjectivity, and is therefore a sign of a person" when the tool is an extension of the agent.[20] And this ability to use tools rests on the "intuition of the agentive-self through the instrumental relationship we humans, of all creatures, have to our bodies due to the properties of the hand."[21]

The hand is the first of our tools for finding more "efficient means of interacting with the world."[22] This fact presupposes not only the agency behind the use of the hand as a tool but also the fact of *interactions* with other objects/subjects in a common ontological space that we call the world. So to be an agent means to be in *interactive relation* with other objects, and if the world contains more than just me as agent, then some of those other objects will be agents as well. And if God is to be considered an agent, even God would need a common ontological space in which to interact with other agents (even though they may all be, with respect to their origins and maintenance, God's creatures).

Tallis argues that if we are agents we cannot be explained completely or exhaustively in non-agential terms. We are certainly material organisms but, he insists, we are not *only* material organisms. "Humans are both organisms that have come into being through processes that are seen throughout evolutionary history and at the same time agents, persons, selves, who cannot be explained satisfactorily in biological, or indeed physical, terms."[23] Tallis does not deny that human beings emerged from a biological substratum but insists that there is a "fundamental gap between instinct-driven organisms and reason-invoking, choosing humans."[24] The problem of explaining agential action emerges when the actions of freely acting agents are subject solely to reductionist instinct-driven organic evolutionary theories. Tallis claims that "the millions of years during which we have progressively deviated from animals is enough to make most organism-based explanation of our behaviour (as opposed to our kidneys' behaviour) totally useless. A description of the roots does not capture the rustling of the leaves."[25] None of this, of course, denies that the efficacy of our

20. Ibid., 231.
21. Ibid., 259.
22. Ibid., 268.
23. Ibid., 273.
24. Ibid., 311.
25. Ibid.

actions depends upon and presupposes the organic and physical infrastructure into which they are inserted. "There is a constant intercutting between conscious intention, bodily mechanisms and the laws of physics. It is this that the grasping hand . . . . first brings to consciousness."[26] In fact, what Tallis calls the "mystery of how it is possible that the 'I do' can stand at the centre of some of 'This happens' gathers force as we become more and more aware of the continual presence of natural laws and of their particular manifestations in our bodily mechanisms behind, before and within our actions."[27]

Tallis is in complete agreement with Macmurray's notion that the sense of the self as agent is prior to and more basic than the sense of the self as thinker. "The development of the sense of oneself as an agent, acting directly or indirectly through the instrument of one's body, lies at the root of the emergence of human self-consciousness and the sense of self. 'I act (deliberately) therefore I am' has always seemed to me to pin down the basis of the sense of the self better than 'I think therefore I am'. . ."[28]

Before leaving *The Hand*, we might note one or two oblique references to God in Tallis's work. He notes that freedom to act presumes, as we have already observed, a "world" in which the actions will occur. "Freedom has to be conditioned in order for it to have particular content, for it to be exercised. Agency has to act upon, and within, a framework composed of, states of affairs it has not chosen. At its deepest level, we have to be 'a given something' [a theme he will develop in his next book *I Am*] we have not chosen to be in order to that we should act on choice." In other words, there have to be what he calls "*enabling constraints* without which the agent would lack an agenda. The things that seem to determine us from outside our agency are also those things that make the notion of exercising agency meaningful."[29] Tallis seems to be saying that action is impossible if there is no external other (or panoply of others in an ontologically constrained world) in which the action is to take place. If there were literally no resisting objects and no ontological conditions (such as time, space, and matter) then there would be nothing in relation to which the act could take place. Given this fact, and presuming the traditional or classical view of God as not limited by anything "other" than Godself, Tallis observes in passing that this is why "it is difficult to think of God as free because He has nothing to be free from, nothing to be free about, nothing to free Himself towards. No wonder he has such a dull history: he is little other than

26. Ibid., 325.
27. Ibid.
28. Ibid., 286.
29. Ibid., 291.

a crystal of frozen, abstract attributes."[30] As we observed in our exploration of the implications of ontological dualism and monism, their metaphysical approaches to God do, in fact, wind up precisely in a view of God as so free from everything that God becomes nothing more than a frozen abstraction to whom no attributes can be ascribed. If God is to be truly relational, God must stand in some "relation to and with" other beings and this means within some kind of common ontological space or structure in which the mode of their interaction is both free within enabling constraints and effective in so far as it seeks to modify the other with whom it is in relation. In this sense, God will have to be "limited" in the way any agent-in-relation is limited by the freedom and existence of the other with whom it is in relation. When this is the case, then God creates a far from dull history. As much of theology and the biblical narrative make clear, God becomes an active, vibrant, and robust contributor to history.

One might, of course, explore the possibility, if one is inclined to a non-dualist/non-monist view of God, that God is the one agent whose repertoire of tools for carrying out God's intentions is virtually (in practice) infinite or unlimited. As finite agents, we have a restricted toolbox of instruments and a limited ability to use them in enacting our intentions in the world; there are many potential instruments in the world we simply are not able to utilize given the limits on our power, imagination, and the infrastructure from within which our acts originate and are deployed. But if God is the creator of the world and is able to act within it as the practical field of God's action, then God would have capacities and possibilities not available to us. If we say these capacities are infinite we don't mean that they are so ontologically "other" than our own that they cannot be conceived. We would mean only that their reach, depth, or degree of power and efficacy is so much greater than ours that we can regard their presence in and availability to God as something that which nothing greater can be conceived.

In the next book of the trilogy, *I Am*, Tallis moves deeper into an understanding of the self as agent. In coming to know ourselves as agents, we get a sense of our individual self "as a subject haunting (using, suffering, enjoying living and being) one's body . . . this, then, is how the hand awakens the intuition of the *agentive subject*."[31] One becomes aware of one's body "as engaged in purposeful activity, as it presents itself in the consciousness of the engaged individual."[32] Calling this awareness that "I am this person, life,

---

30. Ibid.
31. Tallis, *I Am*, 7.
32. Ibid., 16.

consciousness, body" (not a bare and abstract "I am") an "existential intuition" (EI), Tallis says that it "lies at the bottom of every manifestation of (truly) first-person being; without this Intuition, which is unique to mankind, there is no self (or selfhood) and nothing corresponding to personal identity and agency. The existential Intuition is (implicitly) presupposed in them both, which is why it has tended to be overlooked; and this is also why, I believe, philosophers have found selfhood and agency so elusive, with the self apparently melting away on close inspection and agency seeming to have no place in the physical world."[33] Fortunately "...the Existential Intuition lies at the heart of agency, explaining how, in particular, human beings can be 'a point of origin,' a source of true actions, and consequently be able to change the course of nature."[34] As Tallis says later on in the book, "there is an inseparable link between the Existential Intuition and the intuition of agency—'That I am this . . .' and 'That I am *doing* these events' are a twin birth."[35] With the EI "we have a *new point of departure*, in an otherwise boundless material universe of causes leading in all spatio-temporal directions. . . . 'That I am this . . .' plants the flag of 'here' and 'now' and makes our bodies a new point of origin in virtue of which humans are the true 'arche' of those events we believe to be our freely chosen actions."[36] The EI establishes the unique, irreducible particularity of the self (that, of course, immediately establishes a differentiation between one self and all the others). Differentiation is an indispensable condition of interrelational agency. This fact, we might remember, is why the move toward undifferentiated oneness in Meister Eckhart led him to deny the concept of God as an agent.

The EI stands in sharp contrast with the Cartesian "I am because I think." Descartes, from the starting point of the *cogito,* had much difficulty reaching the non-mental STMW in which we as agents are already embedded bodily and engaged *before* (even as a precondition for) beginning to think in the first place. Indeed, Tallis claims that earliest form of the EI "is the body as engaged in purposeful activity, as it presents itself in the consciousness of the engaged individual,"[37] suggesting that the primordial awareness of the self is as an agent whose agency is the primary mode of engagement. He says that the "primordial 'am' is an assumption by itself of a meaty being engaged with the material world. It is the engaged organism assuming itself as 'myself.'"[38] If I begin my

33. Ibid., 23–24.
34. Ibid.
35. Ibid., 292. Emphasis added. Tallis, I believe, slips in using the word "events" because agents originate actions. Events are originated by non-agential causes.
36. Ibid., 300.
37. Ibid., 16.

reflections on the primordial "am" from the standpoint of the EI. I can hardly be mistaken that I *am* this engaged body. It is I who am struggling to *do* something and doing is the heart of agency. Even the cogito argument "truly exists only through being enacted,"[39] the action in this case being that of thinking (the point Macmurray was at pains to make). And in the process of thinking I make assertions about what I believe to be the case. But an "assertion" carries the aura (and reality) of action: to assert something is to *do* something and thus points backward to its origin in and through an action. A self that is only a thinker is a self without a world about which to think. It would be, in effect, a disembodied self without any connection with action in relation to anything beyond itself. "Action would be neither possible nor required."[40]

Tallis does not claim that the self-consciousness that I am this and that I am doing these things emerges full blown at the very beginning of my self-reflection. It is only subsequently that "selfhood and agency differentiate, so that it then makes sense to link together, as if they were separable, the self and its actions, and to attribute the latter to the former."[41] Eric Matthews, writing about the work of Maurice Merleau-Ponty, has said "even our awareness of our own subjectivity is possible only if we are aware of a world that transcends it."[42]

Tallis also claims that "without objects in the 'weighty' sense, it is not clear that there can be a realm of objective truth falsehood beyond that of 'subjective experience' . . ."[43] since there would be nothing outside my thinking by which to judge its truth or falsity. This is not an unqualified acceptance of the so-called correspondence theory of truth or any particular version of pragmatism, but it does suggest that without some reference to a world that has something of its own ontological structure in which we act, the truth of mental conceptions will be difficult to establish.

"The creature woken out of sentience to knowledge awakes to a dangerous world outside of which is incompletely scrutable [sic]. It is not surprising, therefore, that it should arrive at the idea of a 'true' self that is so far 'inside' the body as to be insulated from the threats of the world, and the threats to that body, a self whose existence is potentially underwritten by a transcendent creature (e.g. a God) who is and knows and encompasses the inscrutable

---

38. Ibid., 43.
39. Ibid., 58.
40. Ibid., 121.
41. Tallis, note 34 in *I Am*, 84.
42. Eric Matthews, *The Philosophy of Merleau-Ponty* (Montreal: McGill-Queens University Press, 2002), 84.
43. Tallis, *I Am*, 130.

remainder of the inscrutable world."[44] But, apart from Tallis, we have already seen the consequences of complete inscrutability in the logic of ontological dualism and ontological monism, which eventually collapse into complete unknowing. Not even God can rescue us from that unknowing unless God, too, is not so far "inside" Godself that God cannot have objective and dynamic relations with those beings that are "outside" Godself in the world of relationality, with beings with an ontological independence of each other while still occupying a common ontological space or field in which they interact.

Like Macmurray, Tallis puts a strong emphasis on the physical sensation of touch (as he develops in *The Hand*) as the primordial moment of engagement with what is other than us. It is the sensation of relationality at its most basic: "Touch is of particular interest because, uniquely of all the senses, it has reciprocity built into it: we touch at the cost of being touched."[45] (Might Michelangelo have intuited this when his God at the moment of creation reaches out and touches the hand of Adam?)

But with the existence of the primordial self as agent there necessarily emerges the location of that self in a particular time and place. In order for the self to make any kind of sense of itself, "it has to be impregnated by the past and pregnant with the future . . . 'I' requires an historical context, a temporal depth, for it to be contentful, or for its contents to signify."[46] The EI establishes an original "here" at which the buck starts.[47] And once it starts, a historical narrative is generated.

Acting is the creating of history. Moving beyond anything Tallis has said or even would be sympathetic toward, one might suggest that a God who is actually[48] engaged with what is other than the divine self is necessarily engaged in creating a historical narrative, through actions that occur in time and space and which, with the cooperation (or resistance) of other agents, bring about the completion of the divine intentions.[49]

Macmurray has argued that the non-personal Other is that which does not respond personally to my call to it: "The relation I have with it lacks the mutuality of a personal relation." It corresponds to the non-intentional, non-

---

44. Ibid., 187.
45. Ibid., 192.
46. Ibid., 296.
47. Ibid., 307.

48. Notice how the word "actually" has at its root the notion of "act." To make something real it has to be "actual" or "actualized." Act, agency, and agent are essential to what it means to be real.

49. This reference to narrative history, of course, closely parallels the monotheistic traditions of the West that all rely upon the historical narrative of what they take to be the actions of God in history. The theological implications of this will be taken up in a later chapter.

agent part of myself. When it resists me, it does so not as an agent but passively as a material or organic object. It becomes, in effect, a means for me to carry out my intentions in relation to other agents but is not itself an agent.[50]

All personal relationships seem destined to run into difficulties at some point, for long or short periods of time. If I am rebuffed by the personal other or feel isolated from her, I become egocentric, fearful, defensive, and, in extreme cases, fall into despair. Only if the personal other can break through my defensive shell can I be restored to a loving relationship, assuming I accept the overture. But the restoration of relationality requires an initial breaking away from the other, allowing the negative dimension of relationship (fear) to gain the upper hand. Nevertheless, I cannot be a fully relational being unless I can experience my own identity as an individual self, not simply a dependent self-defining itself solely through the other. If I am to be a full, intentional, and contributing member to the relationship, I must retreat from it temporarily in order to restore it on a different or better basis. In the process, Macmurray insists, I will discover myself as an individual and through that discovery become a more mature and fulsome person. This process involves the crucial notion of *resistance* to the other. Macmurray is quite clear that personal relations do not involve the submerging of the individuality of the persons in relation: they require its enhancement. Only by experiencing and offering resistance to the other can the child discover himself "as an individual by contrasting himself, and indeed willfully opposing himself to the family *to which he belongs*; and this *discovery* of his individuality is at the same time the *realization* of his individuality."[51] This is the "rhythm of withdrawal and return" that is essential for the healthy growth of individuality. (Macmurray notes that this rhythm is as true for societies as it is for individuals and we will take up this issue shortly.)

Temporary withdrawal from the Other becomes the basis of a moral struggle: there is an opposition to be overcome, a conflict of wills to be resolved. This opposition helps the child recognize himself as an individual agent through the experience of encountering an opposing agent who seeks to subordinate him to his will. The Other's will must be met by my counter-will. This clash of wills gives rise to a need for reconciliation, for overcoming the fear of the Other

---

50. John Macmurray, *Persons in Relation* (New York: Humanities Press, 1991) 82. Macmurray believed that organic objects were "persistently ambiguous" in terms of how they are to be conceptually discriminated from other objects. They fall somewhere between the purely mental and the purely material and can be discriminated only in practical terms. The relation of material or mechanical dimensions of reality, and the organic and personal dimensions was originally developed by Macmurray in *Interpreting the Universe*(London: Faber & Faber, 1933).

51. Macmurray, *Persons in Relation*, 91.

without subordinating himself to it in a servile manner by refusing to accept his own individuality and distinctness.

The notion of resistance to an agent's actions presupposes a differentiation between the agent and the objects (including other agents), which the agent encounters in the field in which his or her actions are being enacted. It also presupposes some kind of continuity of the agent from one act to another. Tallis notes that there is no identity without an enduring something, a continuant, to which it might be attached.[52] This is similar to Macmurray's claim that "to be an agent a person must also be a continuant object in the world"[53] and both Tallis and Macmurray echo Thomas Reid who said that "my personal identity . . . implies the continued existence of that indivisible thing that I call myself. Whatever this self may be, it is something which thinks, and deliberates, and resolves, and acts, and suffers. I am not action, I am not feeling; I am something that thinks and acts and feels."[54]

Tallis is not opposed to the notion that our EI and the self-as-agent that it requires emerged gradually over time through a process of evolution. The organisms from which we evolved were at one time without consciousness or will. But at some point we discovered "our ability deliberately or genuinely to *utilize* our body" and in the process we discovered that we can be "a point of true origin, a new beginning in the universe. Bodily self-utilisation transforms hominids' sites of organic events into actors who to some extent shape their own destinies and lead, rather than merely live, their own lives. . . . It is *manipulation* that has awoken the intuition that, among the flow of events, there are some that I *do*."[55] We move from instinctual behavior to "explicitly purposive activity, with a consequent gradual displacement of instinctive behaviour, tropisms and automatic responses to stimuli, by deliberate activity."[56] The sense of agency, according to Macmurray begins at the earliest stages of consciousness. "Self-consciousness, the assumption of the active body as 'I,' and the inchoate sense of agency, are it seems reasonable to conjecture, fused in the most primitive stages of (distinctively) human consciousness."[57] The agent builds upon the organic dimension of the self. As Tallis puts it, "the emergent human agent is built on, or out of, the biological material of the appetitive, active, animal."[58]

52. Tallis, *I Am*, 268.
53. Macmurray, *Persons in Relation*, 39.
54. Qtd. in Tallis, *I Am*, 279.
55. Ibid., 296.
56. Ibid.
57. Ibid., 298.

Macmurray comes at this question by considering the maturation of the baby into a more fully conscious adult agent. In his chapter on Mother and Child in *Persons in Relation* he argues that the child's very survival depends upon maintaining the caring/loving relationship into which she is born. Someone must think for the child until she can learn over time to control her own adaptation to the environment. The child cannot speak in words but the mother interprets her crying or other expressions of discomfort or comfort and the mother must, in effect, act for the child.[59] Until this child can achieve her own agency, her movements are "conspicuously random"[60] and, I would suggest, may well be best described in purely organic, scientific, and even evolutionary terms. The child must eventually discriminate within the field of its senses the different responses that her crying or movements evoke in others. It is only on the basis of this discrimination (dare we say differentiation) that the child can eventually become a self-conscious agent on her own. The child acquires skills to help navigate and negotiate the world in which she is placed. And this acquisition of skills is a cumulative process. But at some stage in the process "we begin to suspect the presence of deliberate intention," a point at which "the child can form an intention and so foresee the end which is his goal, and select a means of attaining it."[61] And so personal agency is born in the child as she moves from mere instinctual response to external stimuli to conscious intentionality.

Tallis places this evolution of self-consciousness and self-agency in the relation of the child's body with the material world. "It is only in the context of first-person being that the material world becomes something in, on, against and for which actions act and upon which there are patients of events. It is the self-appropriation of the body that, ultimately, transforms the material world into circumstances, substrate, opportunity and constraint."[62] This self-appropriation, he argues (very much as Macmurray had done) is the move from pure organic being to personal or agential being. The EI "inaugurates the (never complete) uncoupling of the human person from the human organism, permitting the latter to engage with the natural world on more favourable terms than are allowed to all other creatures. This uncoupling becomes more

---

58. Ibid., 301. This is similar to Macmurray's notion that the "personal" includes the "organic" as its substructure but goes beyond it. See *Interpreting the Universe*.

59. Macmurray acknowledges that men "can do all the mothering that is necessary" and is simply using "mother" because it is more intuitively common to do so.

60. Macmurray, *Persons in Relation*, 52.

61. Ibid., 56.

62. Tallis, *I Am*, 329.

extensive with the growth of objective knowledge out of first-person awareness."[63] And intimately related to this awareness is doing things for a reason, not simply responding organically or even mechanically to stimuli.

An action is more of an action the more it is driven by *reasons*. Possibilities exist only for higher-order consciousness: doing things for reasons separates humans by an ever-widening gulf from the animal kingdom.[64] "It is the expansion, over the generations, of the theatre of distinctively human action that has enabled reasons gradually to displace, override, requisition, biologically inflected causes as the basis of human activity and material causes to be displaced by human intentions. The many-layered human world of explicit reasons, artifacts and institutions buffers human freedom from the deterministic material universe with which it seems to be in direct conflict."[65] Selfhood and agency co-emerge. "Free agents are the origins of their actions but not the causes of them—in the sense of being special (uncaused) causes."[66] Causal explanation by itself is insufficient to explain the way in which agents bring about the realization of their purposes or intentions. In some sense the personal agent uses (without necessarily violating) the causal structures of the organic and physical world (normally explained fully by causal law) in order to *utilize* those laws to attain a rationally chosen end. It is this claim that will be extensively developed in my treatment of Pols.

For both Tallis and Macmurray, agency is the ability to *choose* how to exploit the laws of nature, to subordinate nature to non-natural ends, and it remains distinct from the idea of agency as a supernatural kind of cause. Agents are not solely physical causes of their actions.[67] This point will have significant implications for our understanding of the agency of God in relation to the world in which God presumably acts. For all agents, Tallis argues, agency is a *self-positioning* among causes, "a way of privileging certain events as causes so that we may use them as handles to manipulate the world. In order to act freely, we do not have to be lawbreakers, only law-users."[68] "Self-conscious agency is situated in an almost limitless field of deliberation and explicit purpose."[69] And it is precisely here that Pols's work on the appropriation of the bodily infrastructure of the agent will become essential to developing

---

63. Ibid., 338.
64. Ibid., 304.
65. Ibid., 323.
66. Ibid., 327.
67. Ibid., 309.
68. Ibid., 309–310.
69. Ibid., 321.

the full implications of the notion of the primordiality of agency. For Tallis, "it is only in the context of first-person being that the material world becomes something in, on, against and for which actions act and upon which there are patients of events. It is the self-appropriation of the body that, ultimately, transforms the material world into circumstances, substrate, opportunity and constraint."[70]

Tallis does say that reasons do not "break into the charmed circle of law-like material causation."[71] But as we shall see, this phrasing does not quite do the trick. Law-like material causation is either already porous enough that it admits some "happenings" to take place in the world through rational free agency, or it is a closed causal chain into which some of those things we call reasons or intentions must break in order to bring about their intended effects. If there is no "breaking into" the world of material causation, then where do actions take place? But words like "breaking into" or "intervening in" the world of causality suggest a kind of supernatural power and Tallis rightly flees from such a suggestion. I will argue that intervention or breaking into is, in one carefully nuanced sense, what *all* agents do (both human and divine). But intervention does not mean annulment, displacement, or abrogation of causal law. It means only the appropriate utilization or, as Pols will call it, deployment of causal law for intentional purposes by the agent. Therefore, I will suggest, the concept of *utilization of* rather than *intervention into* the world defined by causal law is a less misleading way of understanding action, including the action of God.

70. Ibid., 329.
71. Ibid., 327.

3

Edward Pols and the Metaphysics of Agency

Completely congruent with both John Macmurray's and Raymond Tallis's views of the agent, the late Edward Pols developed a conception of agency that does three significant things: one, it establishes the ontological primordiality of agency and of the agent who exercises it; two, it rejects the notion that agency can be reduced to its constituent or atomic parts fully explained by a cause-effect relationship; and three, it suggests a way by which agency can be brought into a metaphysically harmonious relationship with the concept of "Being," a concept that points toward a notion of God. I want to explore the foundations and implications of Pols's work on agency as a way of establishing the metaphysical grounding of the notion of God as a personal agent. I am not entirely sure Pols would have agreed with what I want to do with his basic categories and arguments as applied to God, but I completely accept the soundness and conceptual power of his arguments for understanding agency and agent as they exist in the spatio-temporal-material world (STMW). For me, the only problematic aspect of his thought has to do with whether God is best conceived of as *an* agent (without qualification) or whether God is best thought of as the ground of the agency, the power from which agency proceeds and in which all agents participate but is not itself *an* agent. We will take up that issue at the end of our discussion of Pols's view of agency and agent.

At the heart of his work is Pols's conviction that "the most fundamental and concrete sense of power accessible to our intelligence is *power in the sense of agency*."[1] Pols works out the fuller implications of this foundational claim in his 1975 book *Meditation on a Prisoner: Towards Understanding Action and Mind*[2]

---

1. Edward Pols, "Power and Agency," *International Philosophical Quarterly* 11, no. 3 (September 1971): 295. Emphasis added.

2. Edward Pols, *Meditation on a Prisoner: Towards Understanding Action and Mind* (Carbondale, IL: Southern Illinois University Press, 1975).

and in *The Acts of our Being: A Reflection on Agency and Responsibility*[3] (1982), as well as in shorter articles. This reference to power in the form of agency is religiously significant because every credible notion of God presupposes that God exercises power. If, as we said at the beginning of this study, God's efficacy in the world is a crucial dimension of God's being and necessary for God's being worthy of worshipping, then efficacy in the form of agency is foundational for any conception of God. A powerless God is a (literal) non-starter. The question is always not whether but *how* does God exercise power? How does God effect change? How is God able to listen and respond to prayer? How does God affect the world? A non-efficacious God is not a God worthy of being worshipped. So the first religious implication of Pols's conviction is that God must at least exercise power as an agent exercises power (in addition to whatever other kind of power God might exercise). And this drives us immediately back into an analysis of act, agency, and agent as the foundation on which the conception of God as efficacious being (or agent) must rest.

Pols knows that the one of the most baneful legacies of the attempt to secure a rapprochement between classical philosophy and science has been the belief that the best and most complete explanation of occurrences in the world is by reference to intra-mundane causes (within a completely determinate causal nexus). Such an explanation is usually taken to be more basic than explanation by action since action, it is assumed, can always be broken down or reduced into more basic causal "forces" that are in principle fully explained by causal or natural laws. The problem, as Pols sees it, is that within the causal law model (what he calls the Cause-Effect or C-E relation) human agency becomes merely one cause among others, itself an effect caused by something prior to it and thus reducible to explanation by those causes. It has no ontological authenticity or uniqueness that distinguishes it from the events that have no agent-source and that constitute the causal nexus of the STMW. But if scientific causality is essentially physical or mechanistic, then acts have no ontological uniqueness that carries them "beyond" being merely physical or mechanical occurrences under another name. They are nothing more than causes by another name that fit fully within a deterministic C-E schema, having no ontological authenticity of their own that would distinguish them from physical causes within the closed C-E schema. Pols would argue, however, that mechanistic causal law (devoid of consciousness, intentionality, or purpose) is an abstraction from a richer, fuller understanding of how power is exercised in the world. (He does not, of course, claim that all power is agent power since many, perhaps most, things happen in

---

3. Edward Pols, *The Acts of Our Being: A Reflection on Agency and Responsibility* (Amherst, MA: University of Massachusetts Press, 1982).

ways for which a C-E explanation is perfectly adequate. There are both [non-agent caused] events and [agent-initiated] actions.)

The common sense assumption we all make (as rational beings who can comprehend arguments and enact intentions) is that we are agents who do things, things that would not happen unless we did them. Of course, some things just happen to us and we are not responsible for them. Many biological occurrences take place *in* our bodies (e.g., synapse firings) without our intending them. But other things *are* our doings. We are the agents who stand behind them as their authors or originators. We don't need to be shown by argument that we do some things intentionally: we know without having to prove to ourselves that we do these things because, in fact, we do them and take responsibility for doing them. Our sense of agency is rooted in our direct experience of being agents who exercise agency in doing things we intend to do. And in the process of exercising agency we also discover the difference between what we do (acts) and what merely happens (events) without our doing it.

For example, I can choose to blink my eyes rapidly as a sign to my friend to hurry up. Had I not made the intentional choice to blink, my eyes would not have blinked that fast at that moment. But my choice is the beginning, or origination, of an act that tries to realize an intention that informs that choice. However, blinking requires a whole set of movements that I do not consciously choose or control in detail: muscle contraction, synapse firing, microscopic brain movements, and so on. These occurrences (not doings) are well covered by scientific causal law, which is absolutely necessary to explain how these "internal" movements in my body occur: how one biological or neuronal element "causes" another to occur. But this causal explanation of what has taken place in my body in order for my eyes to blink does not cover the "reason" I blinked; it does not take adequate account of the intention behind (and guiding) what the causal factors in the act produced. In short, the act is more inclusive and fuller than the causal elements necessary to its being enacted. The act is only fully explained by reference to the intention that initiated or originated it whereas the normal biologically determined blinking of my eye requires no reference to intention.

Macmurray on Causality

This takes us back briefly to the point Macmurray makes when he observes in *The Self as Agent* the difference between acts and events. Acts, he argues, are performed by an agent who sets out to actualize a possibility that in the absence of the act would not occur. "In action . . . the Agent generates a past by actualizing a possibility . . . To act, therefore, is to determine . . . [and] to determine is to make actual what is, apart from the acting, merely possible. . . . We may therefore define acting as determining the future."[4] What has been determined is the past, which Macmurray calls the field of actuality, whereas the future is the field of possibility.[5] In fact, for Macmurray, "the world is known primarily as a system of possibilities of action."[6] And in acting "the 'I do' is experienced as a felt tension in the Self. . . . a 'tensing' of the Self . . . directed towards the Other. . . . We *intend* a modification of the Other, to be determined by our agency. We *attend to* a mode of the other which is already determinate in order that it might reveal to us the structure of its determination" so that we can effectively bring about a change in it.[7] (Attention in the service of intention is the act of the self's taking time to think about or analyze its field of possibilities so that its subsequent action will be informed by knowledge.) This is what Macmurray calls the rhythm of withdrawal and return, which we touched on in the previous chapter.

Action requires intelligent foresight, rationality, or what Macmurray calls knowledge. Action is "a unity of movement and knowledge . . . knowledge is that in my action which makes it an action and not a blind activity" or, better put, a movement per se.[8] And knowledge includes an "'objective' awareness," an awareness of both the Self and the Other in relation to which it acts.[9] This Other can be either multiple or singular: it is whatever stands over-against and in relation to the agent constituting the agent's field of activity. As we said earlier, this Other presents some kind or degree of *resistance* to the self's action. "Without an other there can be no self. Without a resistance there can be no action. . . .Without an other no action is possible."[10] (This fact will have important implications for the notion of God as agent since to be an agent God would have to have an "other" over-against God constituting the resistance to God's action. This resistance can also encompass cooperating with divine action. But a God who is not differentiated in some way from that upon which God acts could not be an agent.) Macmurray also believes that for genuine action to occur (as opposed to just movement in time and space): "the possibility

---

4. John Macmurray, *The Self as Agent* (London: Faber & Faber, 1957), 134.
5. Ibid., 133.
6. Ibid., 191.
7. Ibid., 171.
8. Ibid., 129.
9. Ibid.
10. Ibid., 142–143.

of action depends upon the Other being also agent, and so upon a plurality of agents in one field of action. The resistance to the Self through which the Self can exist as agent must be the resistance of another self."[11] This is not an obvious claim (since agents often act in relation to non-agents), but its elaboration need not detain us at this point. We need only to retain the notion of the Other (whether personal or non-personal) as constituting some resistance to us in our active relation to it.

This notion of the Other is crucial to the distinction between acts and non-acts, events, movements, or mere happenings. This Other is what Macmurray calls the "continuant" in contrast to the Self as Agent.[12] The "continuant" is the non-agent Other that the agent's action encounters. The act presupposes an agent as its source or originator, but the continuant's existence and configuration depends only on natural causes unless and until it is "taken over" or used by an agent in the pursuit of the agent's intention. Although it may seem counterintuitive, this leads Macmurray to say that acts do not have causes in the strict cause-effect sense. Instead, it is better to say that they have reasons or intentions behind them: events have causes but not reasons as their source. No agent intends the flapping of the mitral valve in his or her aortic system and thus that flapping is an event caused by factors normally outside the intentional control of the agent. What the agent might intend is an operation to repair damage to the mitral valve and that intention results in actions that result in the repair. (And the repair itself requires a thorough knowledge of the causal structure of the aortic system if it is to be successful.)

As Macmurray puts it, an event is an action from which the element of knowledge (reason or intention) has been removed.[13] A cause, on the other hand, is an occurrence without an agent originating it or is the negation of agency. In an act, causes only "transmit" an effect but do not produce it. A cause "is a means through which something else produces the occurrence."[14] In this case the "something else" is the agent acting upon the agent's intention guided by knowledge secured through reflection and returned to engaged action in relation to the Other. Causal knowledge is absolutely necessary to get the repair job done, but it has to be utilized by the agent in acts of repair that are themselves not determined solely by the causal infrastructure that is being deployed by the agent. "Causal explanation only tells us *how* things happen, and not *why* they happen: it describes the course of events without explaining it."[15]

11. Ibid., 145.
12. Ibid., 144.
13. Ibid., 151.
14. Ibid., 153.

In a clear anticipation of both Pols and Tallis, Macmurray says that tools, instruments, or machines "are means for the transmission of our energy, and so in a sense extensions of our own bodies. . . . [T]he question now is a practical one, and the term 'cause' refers to that which we must alter by our action in order to restore our capacity to act through the instrument."[16] The *instrument* (the primordial example of which, according to Tallis, is the hand) is what Pols will call the physical/biological *infrastructure* of the act. These instruments or infrastructures will be reflected conceptually in a natural law explanation of the causal structure of the continuant, using Macmurray's term, until something intrudes or supervenes upon that structure and begins to deploy it toward the realization of an agent's intention. As it is often said (rather blithely, without full awareness of how metaphysically significant it is) natural law predictions of what will occur in the causal infrastructure are always made with the qualification "provided nothing interferes."[17] This is significant because the notion of action in the world (assuming it has not been reduced to an event explained by causality alone) is not troubled by the notion of "interference." My intent to blink my eyes "interferes" with the matrix of causal continuance that would otherwise "determine" what occurs in my eyes in the absence of my intentional act. The religious question, which we will take up in due course, is whether a divine agent "interferes" in the causal structure of the world in a way that is theologically or metaphysically objectionable given the fact that human agents can and do, whenever they act, interfere with the world of continuance under causal law without raising metaphysical red flags or necessarily "violating" causal law.

Pols on Action

Against this background we can now return to Pols's understanding of action. Almost echoing Macmurray (to whom he makes no reference whatsoever in his publications), Pols takes up the relation between action and causality. He asserts that "action is more basic than causality."[18] Causality (which he often calls horizontal or sequential causality[19]) as currently employed in scientific explanation works with the model of a temporal and spatially linked sequence of factors, the ones preceding causing the ones that come after in a causal

15. Ibid.
16. Ibid.
17. Ibid., 158.
18. Pols, *Meditation on a Prisoner*, 15.
19. Edward Pols, "Knowing God Directly," *International Journal for Philosophy of Religion* 45:31–49 (1999): 36.

chain. Any causal explanation will identify the causes and their effects in this linear temporal sequence. Nothing, in this sequence, explains itself. Everything is explained by causes that came prior to an event if a direct cause-effect relation can be found between them. But when we get to an act performed by an agent we need, according to Pols, "an explanation that comes back to [the agent]" and not simply to non-agential causes. The act of the agent cannot be exhaustively distilled into more basic causal relations no matter how important those relations are to the successful realization of the intention which guides the act. Agent explanation is "final, satisfactory, and not to be set aside by any other."[20] This claim is tantamount to what I've called the primordiality of personal agency. The agent exercises what Pols calls "real causality" in a way that distinguishes agent causality from the infrastructure causes that constitute the causal nexus of the continuant. (We shouldn't be confused by Pols's use of the word "causality" here. He is playing off the common understanding that the word "cause" is the most natural term we have to refer to the bringing about of an effect. But what he is looking for is a "cause" that is more than what one finds in the temporal causal nexus constituting the continuant or the material/biological infrastructure through which the agent acts.) As he says in *Acts of our Being*, "there is something self-explanatory about being a rational agent (1): 'rational agency has itself a powerful *prima facie* explanatory value . . . [I]t is because rational agents are *prima facie* causal powers that they can be used in *prima facie* explanation of other things.'"[21]

To explain acts, what we need, according to Pols, is not a linear or temporal chain of causes and effects but what he calls a "hierarchic science" or "vertical causality"[22] in which the act is deployed throughout the infrastructure by the agent from the top down over a period of time (it is temporally-extensive), *utilizing* the sequential causal relations that constitute the "infrastructure" of the act (what Macmurray calls the continuant). The agent exercises power by unifying into a coherent pattern what would otherwise be simply an array of disparate biological and physical units. The agent does not act "before" the act to cause the act and we cannot explain the act by resolving it into a set of particular C-E relations. To think of the act as requiring an act prior to it is to step on the road toward infinite regress. The act is originative: it begins a sequence of occurrences by initiating that sequence. The act then "ripples like a wave through the whole of the spatial region" shaping that region

20. Pols, *Meditation on a Prisoner*, 11.
21. Pols, *The Acts of our Being*, 1–2.
22. Pols, "Knowing God Directly," 36.

over a time span. The act "influences" and pervades the whole spatiotemporal region. "Its pervasiveness is *sui generis*; it pervades the infrastructure by being responsible for (the 'real cause,' or 'true cause', of) the fact that all the elements in the simultaneous region are together in a concourse within which there are no C-E influences."[23]

This is completely in line with what Macmurray might have called the unification of the continuant in service to the realization of the agent's intention. For Pols, the agent is a "power that so unifies a multiplicity of processes and entities that all C-E like connections that we see in them as we attend to them severally are bent together into a pattern."[24] This means that "real causality" must be ascribed to the highest level of the hierarchical system presiding over the infrastructure, not to its subordinate elements or to the first cause in a causal chain.[25] This is a total reversal of the usual scientific reductionism that wants to ascribe causality to the lowest and most basic causal factors in the physical-biological infrastructure. "The unity of an action is so much an exercise of power on and with an infrastructure as to demand the force of the expression 'real cause.' The action, so understood, is not caused, but it *is* a cause in the sense of 'real cause'" and it originates with the agent.[26] Real causality, that which brings something into being or produces a result must be ascribed to the highest level of the hierarchical system.[27] The "real cause" *originating* in agency is very different from the causality *transmitted* by an entity in a temporal causal nexus. The former originates an action that results in an effect; the latter transmits an effect from a prior "real" cause or, more properly speaking, from an agent. Real causality points to the origination of an action by an agent whose act pervades the entire region under the control of the originating act. This is the hierarchical nature of agency.

The Metaphysical Conditions of Ontic Responsibility

Causality and Agency

As a "real cause" the agent is self-explanatory. This leads to Pols's understanding of what he calls the "metaphysical conditions of ontic responsibility" or of "dependence, causal power, and ontic power."[28] These are the conditions of

---

23. Pols, *Meditation on a Prisoner*, 132.
24. Pols, *Meditation on a Prisoner*, 55.
25. Ibid., 65.
26. Ibid., 71.
27. Ibid., 65.
28. Pols, *The Acts of Our Being*, 29.

action, agency, and agent. The first condition asserts that an ontology of acts "must be referred to an entity that acts . . . the unity of the act and the power exercised in it must depend on the unity and power of the agent."[29] A cause within a causal nexus, Pols reminds us, "is a *transmitted* cause; [and] a merely transmitted cause exercises no authentic [or original] causal power."[30] The act of the agent "is nowhere to be found in a nexus of events linked in C-E terms in linear time because his act is everywhere and at every time in the manifold of an infrastructure understood in other terms."[31] This has the crucial implication that acts do not need to fit "into" a causal nexus, and thus the fear of an agent performing an "intervention" into that nexus never really gets off the ground since "intervention" falsely implies the priority of a reductionist causal nexus explanation over an agent explanation. An originative act, or an act-temporal-unit initiated by the agent, transcends the linear-time appropriate to events within the causal nexus and is "ontologically fundamental"[32] or, in my terms, "primordial." Pols calls these "basic" acts, a claim that will be important when we try to relate his understanding of human action to divine action. An act's power is exercised throughout the whole sweep of the act from beginning to end, through what he calls its "act-temporality."[33] The same thing is true of the spatial reach of its power. The power of an act "is pervasive of space in a way analogous to its pervasion of a time-unit."[34]

The unity of the agent is not accessible to a C-E understanding, which focuses instead on the determination of the sublevels that are being unified by the agent, bending them together into a pattern. We do not want to represent Socrates's action "as an anomalous intrusion into a nature that is regulated elsewhere by C-E causality under ontologically absolute general laws." The action by Socrates should be conceived "as a special case, though a grand one, of the general philosophic principle of individual powers exercising 'real causality.'"[35] The control exercised by a cell over its infrastructure cannot be fully understood in C-E terms. "As a 'real causality' it [the cell] will pervade the total pattern of C-E causality, and will pervade it in a way having significant analogies with the way a law, supplementing lower-level laws, would pervade it."[36] This reference to a cell exercising real causality should not mislead us into

29. Ibid.
30. Ibid., 31.
31. Pols, *Meditation on a Prisoner*, 110.
32. Ibid., 121.
33. Ibid., 113.
34. Ibid., 126.
35. Ibid., 59.

thinking that cells are agents. On Pols's developed view even the cell's "real causality" is ultimately under and hierarchically deployable by the action of a personal agent.

"Given any complex system, if we find in it a control level which would not be viable in nature outside that system, we must look upward in the system for the 'source' of its 'real causality.'"[37] "Given any hierarchical system having levels some of which can not exist (in a natural state) independently of the uppermost level of that system, then the 'real causality' operative at any of those levels must be ascribed to the 'real causality' of the uppermost level." Any "nonindependent unit exercising 'real causality' within the unity of the system we call Socrates . . . owes its 'real causality' to the unity of Socrates himself."[38] In other words, "real causality" is found in the agent itself, not in the causes that the agent brings under its control in using the infrastructure to enact its intention.

"Action is more fundamental than C-E causality. . . . The agent is responsible for his acts, and any C-E account of them that obscures this fact is hopelessly abstract."[39] Yet, an act is, in a sense, a "disturbance *in* a structure,"[40] the structure being the "causes without which the [real] cause cannot be the [real] cause"[41] because there would be nothing to deploy or use in the carrying out of the intention. There has to *be* a causal structure if the agent's intentions are to be realized and that structure provides the "internal" causes that the agent puts to use in carrying out or, as Macmurray puts it, transmitting the agent's purposes.

This notion of *disturbance in* a structure might be a better way of stating the way in which actions take place than by using the language of *intervention into* a structure because it does not suggest as strongly the false notion that the action must conform to or be totally absorbed into the causal structure in all respects. Pols admits that acts do "depend in a very intricate way upon stable physical structures" but only in the sense in which "we act in and with our bodies defines a sense in which we are our bodies."[42] Acts require physical (biological) structures for their en-actment but cannot be reduced to the causal elements that comprise those structures since the whole point of an act is to utilize the

---

36. Ibid., 63.
37. Ibid., 64.
38. Ibid., 65.
39. Ibid., 72.
40. Ibid., 74.
41. Ibid.
42. Ibid.

structures to carry out an intention that is not itself the effect of prior non-agent causes.

THE DYNAMIC POWER OF ACTION

There is a "dynamic power" that embraces C-E relations in a temporal unit.[43] Action is a "wielding, by virtue of its 'real causality,' a pattern of C-E relations in a structure; embracing and sustaining those as well as innumerable other C-E-like relations in the unity of its power."[44] An act is "a power that embraces and sustains all these (C-E) linkages, carrying them along in its temporal sweep."[45] "The category of action . . . is more fundamental than that of C-E causality, and . . . the latter can be derived from it."[46] Action takes causality into itself as the means by which it brings about the realization of the intention of the agent whose action it is.

(This is similar to Macmurray's notion that an event's cause only "transmits" an effect whose ultimate origin is in the intention of the agent. And this is the basis for the distinction between what Pols calls an "event-ontology" and an "agent-ontology.") Now lest there be any confusion here, Pols reminds us periodically that "the category of agent is more fundamental than that of action, although obviously inextricably mixed up with it."[47] Actions cannot take place unless initiated by an agent and the "tie between agent and act must be closer than that between cause and effect."[48] (This will suggest, of course, that any talk of divine acts must presuppose a divine agent whose existence as agent is logically necessary for there to be divine acts at all. What "more" might be found in God will be explored later.)

POWER OVER THE OTHER

The second metaphysical condition requires that the agent be able to exert causal power on something other than itself. (This is an echo of Macmurray's notion of the Other, the resistant, the continuant, the panoply of non-agent beings that constitute the objects comprising the field of action.) This requires, therefore, at least a minimal degree of ontological pluralism: there must be more than one agent or external "other": there has to be a field of objects (that will include both agents and non-agents) in relation to which the agent acts.

43. Ibid., 83.
44. Ibid., 85.
45. Ibid., 86.
46. Ibid., 91.
47. Ibid., 72.
48. Pols, *The Acts of Our Being*, 29.

Otherness between agent and that upon which the agent acts is an ontological condition for agency. This will suggest that God must have a field of objects available to God but which are not God ontologically reified *as* that field (as in monism) if God is to act in relation to them. This otherness is also mutual: God must transcend (be ontologically distinct from) that upon which God acts (otherwise God is acting only upon Godself); and those beings upon which God acts must be ontologically distinct from God if they are to stand in relation to each other as agent-object-agent. One can be both agent and object at the same time (though in not the same way) if one is both acting upon and being acted upon by another agent. Action is reciprocal if an agent is acting in relation to other agents. This mutual transcendence or ontological distinction does not necessarily mean that the "natures" of the agents are radically or wholly different from each other (and thus this view stands in contrast to ontological dualism). The nature of the difference is still to be determined if one of those agents is God. But the notion of mutual transcendence seriously qualifies any notion of God as the only transcendent being or the being whose sole characteristic is transcendence. Complete ontological transcendence is central to dualism, but as we saw earlier, if it is truly an ontological dualism, then God cannot be the only being since dualism implies difference between two things. Therefore, God's absolute otherness is qualified by the reality of an authentic (finite) "other" who stands in relation to God. Thus they are differentiated from each other. And this differentiation ingredient in dualism leads, as we've argued previously, to a desire on the part of some for an undifferentiated oneness in which all otherness is swallowed up in undifferentiated oneness (monism). But in the process, God as agent also disappears and the nexus of Pols-Tallis-Macmurray's arguments will prove to be of no help in framing a concept of God that is both ontologically efficacious and sufficiently mysterious so as to generate worship, devotion, and an answer to the hunger for communion and relationship.

ONTIC POWER

The third metaphysical condition is that of ontic power.[49] This means that the agent exercises causal power over the multiplicity of other entities and events (e.g., neural nets, neurons, micromolecules, cells, organs, organelles, etc.) that contribute to the realization of the agent's act. This ontic power is the "ground of the agent's immanence in its causal power."[50] It is a power that "must pervade the inner complexity of the act—must, that is, pervade

---

49. Ibid., 33.
50. Ibid.

its infrastructure—if the act is to be capable of producing or necessitating something distinct from itself."[51] There must be an ontic distinction between the agent and the infrastructure the agent uses in the deployment of his or her act. The agent is *not* the infrastructure of his or her act but the agent cannot act without the infrastructure. Agents are what Pols also calls "fundamental entities," "primary beings," or "apex beings." These are different ways of calling attention to his claim that agents are uniquely authentic ontic beings the explanation of whom cannot be reduced to something more "basic" than themselves (e.g., as composites of atoms, molecules, organs, organelles, etc.). While they preside over and ramify their actions in an infrastructure, these fundamental entities are not reducible to the infrastructure over which they preside hierarchically. A primary being, according to Pols, is something that is "not completely explicable because [it is] itself a fundamental ground of explanation."[52] And as such, it might seem that a primary being has a certain fundamental mysteriousness about it since it cannot be understood fully in terms other than itself. An explanatory scheme that fails to recognize the ontological uniqueness of agents (such as purely and exhaustively causal schemes) is simply inadequate for explaining the reality of agents and their acts. "However fine-grained your analysis of the infrastructure may be, extending even to the details of its mediation between the world outside an agent and the agent himself, you will not find there the full story of the act itself."[53]

EXPLANATORY ULTIMACY

The fourth metaphysical condition of action by an agent is that of "explanatory ultimacy." Any explanation of an act that leaves out reference to the power of the agent and the agent's intention in acting is inadequate and incomplete, no matter how well it explains the elements comprising the infrastructure without which the act cannot be completed. And this fourth condition leads to a fifth one, namely "explanatory opacity."[54] For Pols, this means that whatever is ultimate cannot itself be explained by something other than itself. In the case of acts and agents, Pols argues, "a radical pluralism of acts would give us the necessary explanatory opacity."[55] This would make each agent *causa sui*. And while this is true for each agent with respect to his or her own acts, it does not

---

51. Ibid.
52. Edward Pols, "The Ontology of the Rational Agent," *Review of Metaphysics* 33, no. 4 (June 1980): 702.
53. Edward Pols, "Human Agents as Actual Beings," *Process Studies* 8, no. 2 (Summer 1978): 111.
54. Pols, *The Acts of Our Being*, 36.
55. Ibid.

explain why or how there are agents in the first place or how they originate. "And so we are back with something or other out of which agents spring and upon which, for all their explanatory ultimacy and explanatory opacity, they must be dependent."[56]

Because this points directly toward some concept of Being or God, we will postpone its exploration until we can take up the question of God more fully. But for the time being, it is sufficient to note that, according to Pols, "there is something in the development and activity of the agent [that] should be inexplicable except by calling attention to the fact that the agent indeed did thus and so. After all details of the infrastructure have been given a partial explanation; after a causal analysis in terms of all the powers that condition it or otherwise contribute to it has been given; after all causal influences from the physical environment, from society, and from training have been considered . . . there must remain some features of the agent-in-act that are inexplicable in the sense that no explanatory technique can further illuminate what is expressed in the statement that the agent acted in just that way. Otherwise agency is inauthentic in the sense that it is not what it purports to be."[57] (I will suggest shortly that these notions of explanatory ultimacy and opacity can be applied to God and to that extent allow divine action to be mysterious and explanatorily opaque without being any less real for all that.)

Partial Determinateness

The sixth ontic condition is that of "partial determinateness." The agent must be determinate to some degree but also indeterminate to a degree "so that the development of an act can begin in partial determinateness, gradually resolve what is indeterminate, and end in full determinateness."[58] There must "be enough" of an already existing agent located in some kind of ontic space with some pre-existing underlying identity or character from which the agent's acts will originate. The agent has to have some degree of prior determinateness or settledness simply in order to act in the first place. Actions originate from a locus; they do not simply bring themselves into existence out of nowhere. Therefore, the agent must have at least a minimal degree of determinateness to form the locus for originating acts. This determinateness, however, need not be total or complete. Agents grow and evolve over time as both a result of their own actions and the actions of others upon them. This is similar to Macmurray's notion that acting is determining the future by acts in the present. Pols reminds

---

56. Ibid., 37.
57. Ibid., 37–38.
58. Ibid., 38.

us that such determination of possibilities can only occur if the agent is to some extent already determinate, that is, settled, factual, and structured so as to be an originator of an act of further determinations in the world. In short, the agent must be able to transcend itself (since it is not predetermined in all respects but has some freedom to initiate actions) but not in radical isolation from what its existence depends upon or from the character it has already created through its previous actions.[59] Pols argues that the agent "becomes in his acts: but his becoming is the unifying power in each of his acts and the unification of all of them."[60]

At the same time, in a gesture toward the mystery of agency, Pols says that the agent is never fully exhausted or revealed through his or her acts. "All the while he links together a number of sub-acts in the unity of a superordinate act, [the agent] may be profoundly 'elsewhere' in the sense that he either withholds or is unable to express something of what he nevertheless in some sense 'is.' This 'potential' dimension of the reality of the agent, however difficult it may be to understand and articulate in language, is enough to warn us that the category 'act' is less fundamental than the category 'being,' even though the two categories stand in mutual support."[61] This should suggest two things about God if we wish to extend Pols's analysis to divine agency: first, that God's mystery is reflected in the fact that God never fully exhausts Godself in God's actions, that God always retains a potentiality for further action (and therefore further revelations of the divine self) in the future; and second, that there may be a way to link the primordiality of the notion of act/agency/agent to a more abstract notion of being without sacrificing the uniqueness of action as a basic category of explanation.

THE HIERARCHY OF AN ACT

Now given these metaphysical conditions for action by an agent, we need to see more precisely how an "originative" act occurs in Pols's scheme and how it escapes from complete causal reductionism. This means a return to the notion of a hierarchical organization of factors within an act. Pols sometimes call this the "enframing" power of an act that "embraces and carries along in its temporal sweep a host of C-E connections."[62] The power of the agent "permeates" the infrastructure of the act[63] and wields it into a unity that it would not have

---

59. Ibid., 44.
60. Pols, *Meditation on a Prisoner*, 315.
61. Ibid., 317.
62. Ibid., 76.
63. Ibid., 90.

absent the unifying power of the agent. But the entities of act or agent can, for particular purposes, be analyzed into a multiplicity that is not that entity (e.g., into events that are not acts).[64] And our reason or intelligence "is equipped to recognize unities that are authentically unities even though analysis may find a variety of multiplicities within them. . . . [T]he unity of an act, and consequently the unity of an agent, [is] a power pervading the multiplicity of an infrastructure, and [is] to be distinguishable *as* a unity *from* that multiplicity to just the extent that its power *unifies* that multiplicity."[65] As such, an act is not explained solely in terms of C-E relations but supervenes on (not intervenes in) them and subordinates them to its unifying power.

The act of the agent then "ramifies" in the sub-acts that constitute the infrastructure of the act through which the agent is instantiating his or her intention in the world. Each originative act, no matter how long, has an "absolutely seamless unity as over against the sub-acts it unifies."[66] Within or under an originative or basic act, there may be any number of these sub-acts, each originative at its own level. Any act that ramifies in the sub-acts that it unifies "will stand to each of the sub-acts much as an agent would stand to a set of successive acts we attributed to him as to an entity with an ontological status more fundamental than the acts themselves."[67] And the infrastructure includes all the physical and biological functions and processes that take place within the persistent physical/biological structure of the body of the agent.[68] The act is a "power so permeating the spatiotemporal manifold of the infrastructure as to unify it—the unification being precisely the full concreteness of the act."[69] Pols calls the relation between the agent and the agent's infrastructure an "asymmetrical" one.[70] "Any act is asymmetrically identical with its sub-acts and so is continuous as over against their multiplicity."[71] This permits the life of Socrates to be considered as an act if it has a seamless unity.

Supervention

The power of the agent's act, as Pols puts it, "orders, disposes, uses, deploys, shapes, binds together, wields the multiplicity of the spatiotemporal elements

---

64. Ibid., 92.
65. Ibid., 93.
66. Ibid., 99.
67. Ibid.
68. Ibid., 103.
69. Ibid., 105.
70. Pols, "Human Agents as Actual Beings," 109ff
71. Ibid.

that make up the infrastructure."[72] The infrastructure is "all the functions and processes that take place within the persistent physical structure of the body."[73] In short, the act is superordinate over or supervenient upon all the elements it wields into a unity. In this sense there is an "identity" between the act and its infrastructure, a "power-relation" between the "one" and the "many" it unifies. "The act "is" its infrastructure by being "in" it, by exercising its power on and by means of the infrastructure, by unifying the infrastructure in a power-unit. The infrastructure, on the other hand, "is" the act by being the multiplicity that is unified by it. . . . [T]he 'relation' between an act and its infrastructure is *sui generis* [and as such] is the defining feature of all those hierarchical entities in which nature is so rich."[74] This relation is asymmetrical, of course, because the infrastructure is not itself the act or the agent that is using it. The act supervenes upon (not necessarily "intervenes" in) all the parts of the infrastructure by governing them according to a unifying and controlling intention, but they do not, in return, supervene upon and control the agent. The unity of the act brings the causal structure into itself as the tool of its instantiation rather than having to fit itself into a causal structure from which it stands apart prior to the action. The act needs these elements of the infrastructure to carry out the intention of the agent whose act is it, and it can be "effective on the uttermost multiplicity of the infrastructure only through the mediation of many subordinate levels."[75] The full realization of the intention guiding the act depends upon the elements it binds together in the infrastructure, but they would not have the power they do unless the act supervened upon them. The concept of *supervention*, which makes sense only in a hierarchical schema, may turn out to be more useful in the discussion of God's acts than the concept of *intervention*, which is often used to explain how God acts in an "otherwise" closed causal nexus of intramundane worldly events. An intervention presupposes the primacy and universal sweep of a cause-effect schema into which something "alien" intrudes from the outside. But Macmurray and Pols both object to the universality of the causal schema, as we have seen, when it claims explanatory ultimacy over those things that are really and primordially acts of an agent. And an intervention runs the risk of being seen as something that contradicts causality by failing to "fit into" the causal nexus in a smooth and seamless way. I believe this risk can be avoided by an appropriate understanding of intervention, but it might be better, as I will

72. Pols, *Meditation on a Prisoner*, 105.
73. Ibid., 103.
74. Ibid., 106.
75. Ibid., 140.

argue in the discussion of divine acts, to use the conception of supervention instead. A supervention does not contradict causality but brings it *under* a hierarchical explanation grounded in the primordiality of an agent's act that utilizes or deploys a causal infrastructure in the completion of its intention.

In fact, as we descend through the lower levels of the infrastructure, we find that they are increasingly "heavy with the weight of mechanism."[76] It is not surprising that an act originating in the free choice of the agent to blink his or her eyes must deploy infrastructure mechanisms that, in themselves, are devoid of choice and intentionality and are thus more fully susceptible to a complete causal explanation (as long as the originating factor of choice is left out of the account). An act takes place by means of a bodily structure and as a disturbance *in* a structure,[77] but it is not reducible *to* that structure since, to use Pols's word, it "supervenes" on that structure. The "enframing" power of an act embraces and carries along in its temporal sweep a host of C-E connections without being reduced to them.[78]

Now, on the basis of this understanding of action, we need to see whether there is a coherent notion of an apex being or supreme agent whose enframing power embraces the whole of the cosmic order—in short, a God who is primordially an agent, and whose actions are fundamentally determinative of what other agents can do in relation to God.

---

76. Ibid., 168.
77. Ibid., 74.
78. Ibid., 76.

4

The Metaphysical Conditions for God as Agent

God as the Exemplification of the Power of Being

To be a personal agent, God must be capable of acting in the world. A fuller exploration of *how* God acts will be taken up in the following chapter. But first we need to establish the metaphysical conditions necessary for God to be an agent while also being the source of the agency and being of all other agents. If Edward Pols is correct, the reality of God as agent must not conflict with the notion that God must also be what Pols calls an Apex Being or Being Absolute, in whom the power of agency for all other agents must be found and from whom that power emanates or derives. For Pols, God must be both Being and the *power* of Being. And, if power is always in the form of agency, then God must be the supreme agent from whose power of agency all other agents exist and in whose power of agency they participate. Unfortunately, Pols does not make this point with as much clarity as I think he should have. He seems reluctant to draw the conclusion that God is not only Absolute Being but also Absolute Agent. I want to argue that God is both the power of agency for all other agents and the primordial agent otherwise known as, to use Pols's term, Being Absolute. Or to put it the other way around, the absoluteness of Being is meaningful only when fully *exemplified* in an Absolute Being who is a primordial personal agent. Absolute Being can only be exemplified in an Absolute Agent.

In this respect, I accept A. N. Whitehead's notion that God is the chief exemplification of the basic metaphysical principles of reality. As such, God exemplifies agency and, by so doing, underwrites and empowers the agency of all other beings.

Pols believes that a full explanation of reality must go beyond what he calls a "radical pluralism of distinct actual beings."[1] Taken solely on their own, all

---

1. Edward Pols, "Human Agents as Actual Beings," *Process Studies* 8, no. 2 (Summer 1978): 110.

fundamental entities form a multiplicity of discrete units. And yet each unit, by exemplifying the power of an agent, is a *participant* power in a more universal power of agency. The question will be whether this power can be conceived any more basically or primordially than as the power of agency exemplified in a supreme and primordial agent. Pols rejects any notion of originative acts "springing from the radical fatality of a wholly discrete and particular 'thisness,' or *haecceitas*."[2] This is the move to a notion of Being or Absolute Being that pushes Pols beyond an explanation consisting solely of reference to *individual* agents. It is not clear, however, whether Pols understands "individual agents" to be finite agents only or if he is avoiding the question of whether God is something other or more than an agent. In this context, his argument seems to suggest that he is referring only to finite agents. Just as an act has no grounding unless it originates from an agent, so agents must originate from some power greater than themselves. He calls this power the U-factor (U for "universal"). It is a "universal source of order of which the laws of nature . . . give us a partial expression."[3] Any scrutiny of the agent as a source of originative acts commits us to the view that all such "act-sources" have a common source. "And this we recognize as that ultimate metaphysical scandal, Being Absolute."[4] The self-identity of a particular agent "is never absolute."[5] The power of particular agents is never entirely self-sufficient or self-explaining. To be a power-center, as it were, requires that the power-bearer, the agent, participate in a power greater than herself, the power of being (or, as I would prefer to call it, the power of agency itself). The human being is "as fundamental as any finite entity in the universe: its continuity massive, though not absolute; its unity a participation in unity and always vulnerable at that, but never merely that of a series of discretes; its self-integration fragile and uncertain . . ."[6] There must be an ultimate source for the self-identity of each particular human agent. This source, or Being, "does not exercise power in the sense in which [the finite agent] may exercise power yet is nonetheless the source of its power. It is precisely what confers upon any particular primary being the character of not being fully determined by the other members of a context of particular primary beings, however wide. It is what makes a rational agent capable of acts that are not fully explicable by explanatory procedures that dismiss the categories of agent and act. . . . [I]t is

---

2. Edward Pols, *Meditation on a Prisoner: Towards Understanding Action and Mind* (Carbondale, IL: Southern Illinois University Press, 1975), 319.

3. Edward Pols, *Mind Regained* (Ithaca, NY: Cornell University Press, 1998), 123.

4. Pols, *Meditation on a Prisoner*, 319.

5. Pols, "Human Agents as Actual Beings," 111.

6. Ibid.

what makes radical pluralisms ultimately unacceptable, since it is what all these primary beings share."[7] A radical pluralism is, presumably, a set or context of discrete beings possessing no common source of their being or agency and thus pluralistically separate and distinct from each other.

This Being Absolute, the source of their being and power, is compresent with all the finite agents and makes possible their action in the world. Thus, "if there are particular primary [finite?] beings that exercise power in action, then they do so by virtue of their status as participant powers . . ." The "primary being or one of its acts is the bearer of a Being that transcends it." [8] Pols admits a certain "ontological mystery" here: it is the mystery of the "concrete particular whose very particularity includes a union with and dependence upon a general, common, or universal power."[9] But the question is whether this general, common, or universal power is itself a primordial agent from which the power of agency flows or in which it is fully instantiated or exemplified, or is it something other, something that is not primordially an agent? Is this the mystery we have been looking for in the primordiality of agency, act, and agent or is it a conceptual confusion unnecessary to the completion of Pols's project? Can we simply think of the Absolute Being as Absolute Agent? What is to be gained by dropping or excluding the primordiality of agency from the meaning of Absolute Being?

The individual or fundamental (finite?) agent, Pols insists, "comes out of Being." The agent's unity, power, and order is a "shared one: it participates in, [and] is a partial expression of, the unity of Being."[10] Each fundamental being is a 'power instance' of a common One.[11] This One or Being, for Pols, is God. It is a "One whose power ramifies in all multiplicities."[12] God is the U-factor in our experience, that which transcends each of the particulars that participate in it.[13] Pols insists that this notion of participation is not the Platonic notion of participation in a conceptual form but rather "the participation of a particular entity in a unity/universality."[14] The relation between the one finite agent and the many acts over which she presides is paralleled by the relation between the One Being that is universal and the many beings that participate in it. This is

---

7. Edward Pols, "The Ontology of the Rational Agent," *Review of Metaphysics* 33, no. 4 (June 1980): 708–709.
8. Ibid., 709.
9. Pols, *Meditation on a Prisoner*, 332.
10. Ibid., 319.
11. Ibid., 332.
12. Ibid., 327.
13. Pols, *Mind Regained*, 119.
14. Ibid.

no radical pluralism of Ones but a "plurality of Ones that share in a universal (thus transcendent) One."[15] But is this transcendent One also and primordially an agent, and if not, then what is it, and what is its relation to agency?

I believe that the notion of "participation" could be an obstacle to understanding Pols's intent unless we carefully define it. The mysticism of undifferentiated oneness, strikingly exemplified in Meister Eckhart, understands participation as the ultimate *identification* of all (only apparently different) entities in one entity or oneness, per se. But if we define participation simply as the receipt of a power of being that originates in the act of an universal agent (or power) then we don't fall into the trap of non-differentiation and thus leave open the door for conceiving of God as an agent differentiated from all other agents (and beings) by virtue of God's exercise of ultimate power in bringing them all into existence in the first place and sustaining them. It is not overly difficult to think of my act of swearing an oath as an act that "participates" in and emerges from myself as the agent who swears. The act is an extension of myself and thus participates in my power. My power "includes" the whole of that arena in the world that my power affects.

The Apex Being

Pols uses the term "apex being" in this context. An apex being is One "but its self-identity includes the multiplicity of its infrastructure beings and so is also Many."[16] Pols admits the mystery of trying to articulate with complete precision the notion of the universal One, the apex being who includes all other beings within its enframing universality (but that is presumably not *identical with*, in an undifferentiated oneness, all the beings that participate in its power of being or agency). It is a mystery because we cannot say *why* it is so, but we "must simply acknowledge our dependence [on the apex being] and acknowledge also that dependence does not exonerate us from the obligation to act as though everything depended on us as particulars."[17] Pols is less than fully clear here about how an apex being can "include" a multiplicity of other beings that participate in it without becoming identical with them or without retaining an identity that is in some primordial sense distinct from them.

Pols address the question of God directly in his article "Knowing God Directly." He recalls that his first serious reference to God was under the rubric

---

15. Ibid., 135.
16. Edward Pols, "Knowing God Directly," *International Journal for Philosophy of Religion*, 45:31–49 (1999): 35.
17. Pols, *Mind Regained*, 136.

"common formative power."[18] This power is then described as the U-factor, the factor of unity and universality, limited only by "its immanence in a particular being or particular situation."[19] This immanence is another way of saying that each P-factor (each particular being) "shares in *the* U-factor, not *its* U-factor, and the union of particular and U-factor is seamless in the sense that we cannot separate the two without producing abstractions—mere (particular) universals on the one hand, mere particulars on the other."[20] The U-factor is a "unifying causal power" and is immanent in each P-factor. This means that the U-factor transcends the particular but is present in all of them in the form of power. In short, we find in each act or agent a "union of U-factor and P-factor that is essential to our rational awareness of act or agent and essential also to the functioning of such things." The U-factor "possesses the agent in the course of the act."[21] The U-factor grounds both knower and known, the agent and that upon which the agent acts, because both participate in it as the common formative power that enables them to be and act in the first place.

Pols says that the U-factor that manifests itself in all primary beings "is not itself a finite primary being."[22] That would make it just one particular alongside other particulars. And it wouldn't explain the universal power that enables particulars to be and to act. So the question is whether the U-factor or God is a non-finite primary being that is nonetheless an agent or if it is something entirely beyond the categories of agent and agency. And here again Pols is less than clear. The U-factor is "something that is at once universal and a causal power that is creative of primary finite beings in the sense that in its union with the infrastructure of the primary being it is intrinsic to *their* causal power."[23] But can a causal power (presumably a vertical causal power exercising "real causality") be anything other than an agent? Can God be both universal and immanent without being *an* agent? If Pols denies that this is the case, has he thereby abandoned his initial claim that "the most fundamental and concrete sense of power accessible to our intelligence is power in the sense of agency"?[24] Is God an agent or not? Given everything that Pols has said about agency, I see no reason to deny that God is the primordial Agent. God, for

---

18. Pols, "Knowing God Directly," 32.
19. Ibid., 43.
20. Ibid.
21. Ibid., 45.
22. Ibid., 47.
23. Ibid., 48.
24. Edward Pols, "Power and Agency," *International Philosophical Quarterly* 11, no. 3 (September 1971): 295.

Pols, is the *source* of the being and power of action in all agents; the universal power from which proceed all acts and agents and in whose power they are grounded. Such a power need not, I think, be something other than an agent, even though it is the one universal non-finite primordial Agent. In fact, the deployment of power, even the universal power to make possible the existence of all other agents, requires some kind of action on the part of the agent doing the deploying. The reach of God's power is universal (infinite) but that reach is still the reach of an agent. So God's universality, and the power that God exercises to give existence and causal power to all other primary beings, is not in conflict with God's also being essentially an agent. Absolute Being does not, therefore, in my opinion, require that it transcend agency or be anything other than the primordial Absolute Agent. Its primordiality and "divinity" is revealed in the fact that it *exercises* agency over the whole of reality, deploying its power throughout the entire multiplicity of particular powers or agents that participate in it as the source of their power and agency. It gives the power of agency to all other beings by a primordial act of giving. I see no reason for Pols to withdraw from Absolute Being the core notion of power in the sense of agency. So Absolute Being can be an agent, albeit a universal one whose originative act includes or supervenes upon all other beings that, by virtue of their existence as participant beings, constitute Absolute Being's primordial act.

This tracks fairly closely with John Macmurray's notion of God as the infinite personal agent both immanent in existence and transcendent of it.[25] Macmurray reminds us that "transcendent" and "immanent" are terms drawn from the nature of persons as agents and are strictly correlative. All agents are immanent in and yet transcendent of what they do in the sense that their potentiality as agents is not exhausted by what they have done or are doing. For Macmurray, God is immanent in the world because the world is God's act. And, to use Pols's language, the world participates in God precisely because it is God's act. But God is also transcendent because as agent God is always engaged in continual self-transcendence and is not identical to what God transcends. There is no reason not to treat Pols's God in the same way. God is the only agent whose power is capable of being immanent in all other agents whose existence and perdurance is God's continuing act (thus justifying a characterization as "infinite") and by virtue of that fact being transcendent of (and differentiated from) any particular other agents or even the totality of them taken as a whole, at least as long as we understand "transcendence" as relative to the unique ontological status of being-in-relation. This is not the "transcendence"

---

25. John Macmurray, *Persons in Relation* (New York: Humanities Press, 1991), 223.

of ontological dualism. As the common source of agential power for all agents, God is more powerful and efficacious than finite agents but not less than an agent. It is the uniqueness of God's agency that gives them the power to *be* agents as well, though with far more restricted scope for their actions than God's.

I think Pols's language about God as "Absolute Being" borders on the unhelpful in this context, but I believe we can extract from his language the point that God is *the* Apex Being, a non-finite primary being, a fundamental or primordial agent-entity. As such, God's causal reach (the extent of God's agential power) is far greater (literally infinitely greater) than that of any finite entity. It would make no sense to understand God as the source of agency or causal power for agency without understanding God as essentially an agent in and of Godself. Only if this is the case do we avoid falling into the trap of radical ontological otherness (the curse of metaphysical dualism) or of radical non-differentiated oneness (the curse of metaphysical monism) both of which the notion of agency as applied univocally to God is meaningless. Whatever God may be in God's own self—if such a notion is even possible—God manifests whatever God is only through the exercise of power and that requires that God be an agent. If there is a mystery to God in Godself, it lies in a kind of metaphysical black hole on the far side of God's exercise of any agency and is irrelevant to our responsive engagement with God as the agent who has engaged us through God's actions to which God is calling us to respond. Some conceptual mysteries, such as what God is when not exercising the power of agency, are perhaps simply impossible to penetrate and, I would argue, have no practical consequences for our relationship with God. Unless solving these mysteries makes our way in the world any easier, perhaps they are best left quite literally to the imagination. There is more than enough mystery in figuring out why agents choose to do what they do, and this mystery is itself more than enough to satisfy the religious curiosity and more than enough to require our full participation in responding to the divine actions with ones of our own.

We have to admit that thinking of God in this way does in fact entail a commitment to a form of anthropomorphism but not of the kind associated with naïve and primitive beliefs in God as an Olympian-like deity. It will be a more sophisticated anthropomorphism in which God is correctly understood as literally an agent in the same basic sense in which we are agents—beings with the power to effect change in the field of action. This is not primitive anthropomorphism because it suggests a view of God as a fuller, less limited, more inclusive, robust being. The full extent, depth, and reach of God's attributes lie beyond the cognitive and practical range of our capacities, but

Gos is not, as a real agent, entirely *outside* or ontologically *transcendent of* our ontological space. If God acts upon us and calls us to respond with actions of our own, we have to share some common ontological space with God. But if God is the creator of the world and is able to act within and upon it as the practical field in which God exemplifies divine agency, then God would have capacities and possibilities not available to us because of the severe limitations ingredient in our possession and exercise of (only) finite agential power. God would have the maximal degree of the power of agency whose power enables other agents to be in the first place, but God would still be an agent, not something that is "more" than an agent (whatever that might be). And if God acts, God must be capable of acting in the same ontological space as other agents and beings. Otherwise God's actions are either illusory or ineffectual, at least as far as we are concerned, since they would not actually "touch" or engage us. Pols's argument entails that God must at least exercise power as an agent exercises power (in addition to whatever other kind of power God might exercise). And the commonality of the exercise of power by the divine being and human beings, grounded in God as the source of the being and agency of other agents, constitutes the ground of a more mature and developed anthropomorphism.

A Note on Thomas Aquinas and "Act-of-Being"

The concepts of act and being will immediately remind some readers of the language of St. Thomas Aquinas. Despite the similarity of terms, I don't think his use of them directly corresponds to Pols's or mine. Aquinas does refer to God as "Pure Act" and as "act-of-being." Nevertheless, the term "act," taken from Aristotelian metaphysics by Aquinas, has a distinct meaning, which is not that of "action" or agency or agent as Pols, Macmurray, and Tallis have deployed them. For Aquinas, "act" is the full reality of an existing being. It must be contrasted with "potency," which is the potential to become act or fully existing determinate or determined being. Act is the cessation of becoming, of potentiality. In act, something no longer becomes, changes, grows, or develops. And thus, according to Aquinas, only God is beyond becoming, only God is fully realized without any potentiality at all. This assumes that change is debility, a "lack" of fullness; and in the classical view of God, that is in fact what is assumed. Thus only God is "pure" or full Act. God is also pure act-of-being because only God can make a substance actually exist or "be." As Etienne Gilson puts it, "substance itself . . . exists only in virtue of a further . . . supreme determination, its very act of being. In this sense, the act-of-being is act of the form . . . that which makes the substance to be a 'being,' as having actual existence."[26] God's act-of-being is different from all the rest because only God exists necessarily. Aquinas, however, is reluctant to describe God as "an Agent." Agency, understood as Pols, Macmurray, and Raymond Tallis do, presupposes a *relationship* between agent and that upon which, or in harmony with which, the agent acts. This relationship sees agency not as a pure act in which becoming has ceased but rather as an "interaction" between differentiated beings, each of whom "acts" in order to attain something not already present to or included in it. In Aquinas, act comes closer to suggesting the cessation of "acting" as normally understood. God does not act in and upon the world because God is Pure Act and beyond (transcendent of) the reality of other objects with whom God might have a relationship. As Aquinas says, God has no relations with anything *outside* God's own self since all relations participate 'in' God.

What we can take from Aquinas, which parallels Pols, is that there must be something that gives being to all that exists other than or different from itself, and in whose power of being they participate. But my argument is that it is metaphysically more appropriate and religiously more satisfying to think of God not as "act-of-being" but as the primordial agent whose acts bring beings into existence and with whom God can have ongoing transactional relationships.

One consequence of the mature anthropomorphism I am advocating is understanding God as acting *within* a world common to God and other agents. Tallis has said that there have to be what he calls "*enabling constraints*" without which the agent would lack an agenda. The things that seem to determine us from outside our agency are also those things that make the notion of exercising agency meaningful."[27] Action is always action in a context, in a relationship to other agents and beings upon whom one's action impacts. This requires God's actions to fall into some context in which there are other agents (as well as non-agents) upon whom God's actions must have an impact and make a difference if they are to be truly efficacious.

RESISTANCE AND RELATIONALITY

This leads us to Macmurray's crucial notion of resistance as essential to relationality. To be an agent God would have to have an "other" over-against God constituting, to use Macmurray's term, the *resistance* to God's action. (Resistance does not mean only *opposition to* but can also encompass *cooperating*

---

26. Etienne Gilson, *The Christian Philosophy of St. Thomas Aquinas* (New York: Random House, 1956), 32–33.

27. Raymond Tallis, *The Hand: A Philosophical Inquiry Into Human Being* (Edinburgh: Edinburgh University Press, 2003), 291.

with divine action provided that divine and human actions are not absolutely identical.) But a God who is not differentiated in some way from that upon which God acts could not be a divine agent. These metaphysical conditions rule out absolute ontological transcendence and complete undifferentiated monism. As agent, God is one being alongside other beings—albeit one in whom they participate as the source of their agency. That is the basic, primordial fact of divine existence. But in itself it doesn't tell us what degree and scope of power God possesses nor what personal qualities God's exercise of that power reveals.

Moving beyond anything Tallis has said or even would be sympathetic toward, one might suggest that a God who is actually[28] engaged with what is other than Godself is necessarily engaged in a historical narrative, with actions that occur in time and space and which, with the cooperation (or resistance) of other agents, bring about the completion of the divine intentions. Given this fact, and presuming the traditional or classical view of God as not limited (or resisted) by anything "other" than Godself, Tallis observes in passing that this is why "it is difficult to think of God [in the classical view] as free because He has nothing to be free from, nothing to be free about, nothing to free Himself towards. No wonder he has such a dull history: he is little other than a crystal of frozen, abstract attributes."[29]

If God is to be truly relational and free, God must stand in some "relation to and with" other beings and this means within some kind of common ontological space or structure in which the mode of their interaction is both free within enabling constraints and effective in so far as divine action modifies the other with whom God is in relation. In the spirit of a mature anthropomorphism, this means that God's actions must occasionally be "alongside" the acts of other agents, even while, as the power of agency itself, God empowers their agency. In this sense God will have to be "limited" in the way any agent-in-relation is limited by the freedom and existence of the other agents with whom it is in relation. God cannot be both relational and, at the same time, completely undifferentiated or absolutely transcendent of those other beings.

This means that God must have a field of objects available to the efficacy of God's acts but that are not themselves ontologically identical with God. The otherness of objects in this field is essential to any notion of agency and that includes the notion of God as agent. But the otherness is also mutual: God must transcend (be ontologically distinct from) that upon which God acts (otherwise

---

28. Notice how the word "actually" has at its root the notion of "act." To make something real it has to be "actual" or "actualized." Act, agency, and agent are essential to what it means to be real.

29. Tallis, *The Hand*, 291.

God is acting only upon Godself); and those beings upon which God acts must transcend (be ontologically distinct from) God if they are to stand in relation to each other as agent-object-agent. One can be both agent and object at the same time (though in not the same way) if one is both acting upon and being acted upon by another agent in the relational dynamics of interaction. Action is reciprocal if an agent is acting upon other agents and they upon the agent. This mutual transcendence does not necessarily mean that the "natures" of the agents are radically or wholly different from each other. The nature of the difference is still to be determined if one of those agents is God. But the notion of mutual transcendence seriously qualifies any notion of God as the only transcendent being or the being whose sole characteristic *is* transcendence, per se. Complete ontological transcendence is central to dualism but, as we saw earlier, if it is truly an ontological dualism then God cannot be the only being since dualism implies difference between two things unless it is a dualism between the real and illusory, in which case it devolves into undifferentiated oneness. Therefore, God's absolute otherness is qualified by the reality of authentic (finite) "others" who stand in relation to God. Thus they are differentiated from each other. And this differentiation ingredient in dualism leads, as we've argued previously, to a desire for an undifferentiated oneness in which all otherness is swallowed up. But in the process, God as agent also disappears and the nexus of Pols-Tallis-Macmurray's arguments will prove to be of no help in framing a concept of God who is both ontologically efficacious and sufficiently mysterious as to generate worship, devotion, and a hunger for communion and relationship.

We will now take up the question of *how* a divine agent whose power of agency makes it possible for there to be a world *can act* in that world and subsequently the question of how uniquely divine acts can be discerned from historical narratives and personal experience as having happened.

5

How Can God Act in the World?
Divine Action and the Infrastructure of the Socio-Temporal-Material World

> *If God is the primordial agent, then how, in fact, can God act in the world?*

If Edward Pols is right, then we must start our understanding of divine action with his claims that God's power "must pervade the inner complexity of the act—must, that is, pervade its infrastructure—if the act is to be capable of producing or necessitating something distinct from itself . . ." The divine act must preside over, ramify in, unify, deploy, pervade, supervene, be superordinate over, and govern all that falls under its sway and exercise of power. God's act "enframes" all that is unified within it and grounds the powers that act at subordinate level within the structures that are being unified and deployed. This "enframing" power of an act "embraces and carries along in its temporal sweep a host of C-E [cause and effect] connections."[1] The power of the agent "permeates" the infrastructure of the act[2] and wields it into a unity. If God is an agent, then God's action is neither reducible to the infrastructure nor completely independent of it. The infrastructure is the *means* by which the divine intentions are realized. Any act that ramifies in the sub-acts that it unifies "will stand to each of the sub-acts much as an agent would stand to a set of successive acts we attributed to him as to an entity with an ontological status more fundamental than the acts themselves."[3]

---

1. Edward Pols, *Meditation on a Prisoner: Towards Understanding Action and Mind* (Carbondale, IL: Southern Illinois University Press, 1975), 76.
2. Ibid., 90.

To put this conception of divine action to work, we can begin with the most vexed and problematic way of thinking about God as acting in the world. This way centers around the notion of divine action "interfering" or "intervening" in the causal structures that constitute the physical world. The problem with this notion of interference, however, is that it suggests that God must somehow "break into," intrude upon, and in the process, "violate" the natural or causal laws by which we "normally" understand the occurrences in the world. But there is a two-fold problem with attempting to eliminate the notion of interference as applied to action: first, if taken literally and carried to its logical conclusion, then there would no such thing as human action in the world. Second, interference suggests that actions must somehow "fit into" an already closed, fixed, and irreducible nexus of events that is completely and exhaustively understood in causal terms in the absence of actions. But if there are human actions in the world, then it is a logically consistent step to understand divine action in the same way we understand human action (while at the same time not identifying one with the other). In order to make this understanding plausible, it is necessary to challenge the notion that all actions must fit into or be subsumed within the causal nexus.

Most discussions of how God acts presuppose a closed causal nexus within which all occurrences take place and the reductive causal explanation by which they are understood. As a result most contemporary approaches (with some notable exceptions) to understanding divine action in the world look desperately and, I would argue, in vain for the "causal joint" that links God's actions to the effects within the causal nexus that we want to attribute to them. But I believe we are misled from the beginning if we assume that it is contrary to our understanding of actions (whether divine or human) to think of them as unexplainable "interferences" in the causal order, which, by their very nature, conflict with a causal explanation of all that happens in the world. There is a benign notion of interference that is perfectly acceptable, but I will argue that there is an even better way of understanding action that simply bypasses concepts of interference or intervention by utilizing Pols's notion of the agent's hierarchical *deployment* of the causal infrastructure in the realization of his intentions.

THE HISTORY OF INTERPRETATIONS OF DIVINE ACTS IN HISTORY

The history of contemporary attempts to address the issue of God's actions in the world from the point of view of modern science can be traced back to

---

3. Ibid., 99.

biblical scholar Rudolf Bultmann and his highly influential book *Jesus Christ and Mythology*. In that work, he brought the notion of God acting in the world under his concept of "mythology" in the service of his demythologization project. As part of his effort to demythologize the Bible in order to get at its inner meaning (or *kerygma*) he stated, without qualification, that "in mythological [meaning pre- or non-scientific] thinking the action of God . . . is understood as an action which *intervenes between* the natural, or historical, or psychological course of events; it breaks and links them at the same time. The divine causality is inserted as a link in the chain of events which follow one another according to the causal nexus."[4] The only way to conceive of a divine act on the basis of this understanding is as a supernatural miracle: "something not visible, not capable of objective, scientific proof which is possible only within an objective view of the world. To the scientific, objective observer God's action is a mystery."[5] And, it follows, the only way to conceive of a miracle is through an act of faith, since it is not susceptible to a rational scientific analysis. "In faith I deny the closed connection of the worldly events, the chain of cause and effect as it presents itself to the neutral observer." And the paradox of faith is that it "'nevertheless' understands as God's action here and now an event which is completely intelligible in the natural or historical connection of events."[6]

Theologian Langdon Gilkey followed up Bultmann's understanding of divine action by insisting that the concept of the "mighty acts of God" in history is now "empty . . . void since the denial of the miraculous," a denial that follows, in his opinion, directly from a scientific (i.e., causal) view of the world.[7] Theologian Gordon Kaufman most famously brought *finis* to this understanding of divine action when he wrote in 1968 that the notion of a God "who continuously performs deliberate acts in and upon his world . . . has become very problematic for most moderns."[8] Kaufman thought that it was only by *excluding* reference to a divine agent that we can secure knowledge of what happens in nature. Each of these thinkers uncritically presupposes the monolithic and exhaustive power of a causal model for understanding anything that happens in the world.

---

4. Rudolf Bultmann, *Jesus Christ and Mythology* (New York: Scribner, 1958), 61. Emphasis added.
5. Ibid.
6. Ibid., 65.
7. Langdon Gilkey, "Cosmology, Ontology, and the Travail of Biblical Language," *Journal of Religion* 41 (1961): 200.
8. Gordon Kaufman, "On the Meaning of 'Act of God,'" *Harvard Theological Review* 61 (1968): 175.

Nevertheless, in order to preserve some semblance of meaning in "divine action," Kaufman appealed to what he called the "master act" of God. God was not the agent behind *particular* acts *in* history but was instead the transcendent source of the course of history taken as a whole. For Kaufman, this "master act" of God "is not a new event that suddenly and without adequate prior conditions *rips inexplicably* into the fabric of experience, a notion consistent neither with itself nor with the regularity and order which experience must have if it is to be cognizable. Rather, here God's act is viewed as the course of precisely that overarching order itself: it is God's master act that gives the world the structure which it has and gives natural and historical processes their direction. Speaking of God's act in this sense in no way threatens the unity and order of the world as a whole."[9]

Notice here the savagery of Kaufman's language when referring to an action's relation to the causal order: a particular act of God "rips inexplicably" into the world and "threatens" the unity of the world as a whole. There is a deep and abiding dualism at the heart of Bultmann's, Gilkey's, and Kaufman's understanding of divine action. In their view, God is ontologically transcendent *of* the world and, by virtue of God's transcendence, cannot act *in* the world without violating the scientific principles by which the closed causal nexus is understood or without compromising God's radical ontological "otherness." This position echoes and is thoroughly informed by that of Immanuel Kant who applied causal law to our understanding of the phenomena of nature while removing God from the world as a noumenon, incapable of being apprehended or conceived by human understanding. As a result of God's noumenal status, God could not be conceived as having any direct contact with the world. A crucial implication of this view, which is often missed in discussion of divine actions in this framework, is that human actions in the world ought to be just as mysterious, miraculous, and incapable of being accommodated by a scientific understanding. Kant understood this and said the only way to introduce human freedom of action into the world was through "practical" reason—not theoretical reason—leaving human action ultimately mysterious and inaccessible to human understanding. Today, of course, many of us are not strict Kantians. We do accept the view that human actions (assuming that they are not reducible to causally determined events) "break into" or "intervene" in an "otherwise" unbroken chain of causally determined events that constitute the causal nexus of the world. Unless we are strict materialist reductionists, we find a need to speak of actions as occurring without being totally predetermined

---

9. Ibid., 192. Emphasis added.

by a closed causal chain. If they were simply part of the chain, there would be nothing to distinguish them as agent-initiated actions from caused events. As long as we intend to preserve a special place for human action (as distinct from mere causal happenings), we have to find a way to put human action to work in the world without reducing it without remainder (under a different name) to causal events apprehended only through a causal law frame of reference. But if human action can "intervene" into the causal structures of the world without causing theological or metaphysical apoplexy that such human action is an inexplicable "ripping" into or a threat to our understanding of worldly events, then why should divine actions evoke such consternation when they, like all actions, intervene in the *otherwise* closed causal nexus? If distinguishing my actions from predetermined causal events is reasonable, as clearly it is, then distinguishing divine actions from the causal events that occur in the world according to patterns of regularity should be equally reasonable and for exactly the same reasons. Keith Ward notes, "If human action can be integrated with natural causality, there is little reason why Divine action should not also be so integrated."[10] I would only quibble with Ward's claim in so far as Kantian-inspired reductionist accounts of action do, in fact, often fail to integrate human action with natural causality by denying the unique and non-reductionist place of human action in the natural world.

God's acts should be no more or no less "unique" than human acts, though they have greater scope, efficacy, temporal and spatial reach, and are more decisive in the changing the course of history, to name a few. As Thomas Tracy has said, God is that individual in whom the capacities that define agency find their maximal expression.[11] By this argument, God would be the supreme agent who exercises the power of agency to the maximal extent possible. If divine action is mysterious then so *mutatis mutandis* is human action and vice-versa. As Keith Ward accurately observes, "there is no possible answer to the question 'how does he [God] do so [bring things about], any more than there is a possible answer to the question 'How does one raise one's arm?' 'One just does.'"[12] (I would add, however, that Pols provides a perfectly reasonable understanding of action that does not end in a kind of throwing up of one's hands as Ward's comment might lead us to believe.) This is not an explanation of action that reveals the mechanics of the causal joint: it is an explanation

---

10. Keith Ward, *Divine Action* (London: Collins, 1990), 76.

11. Thomas Tracy, "Narrative Theology and the Acts of God," in *Divine Action: Studies Inspired by the Philosophical Theology of Austin Farrer*, ed. Brian Hebblethwaithe and Edward Henderson (Edinburgh: T&T Clark, 1990), 177.

12. Ward, *Divine Action*, 18–19.

that refuses the closed causal nexus as exhaustively defining what counts as an explanation of action. Instead, we can argue, action is far better defined through a hierarchical agent-based utilization of the causal infrastructure that makes agency a primordial, not a derivative, category of explanation.

FINDING DIVINE ACTION IN THE WORLD

Despite the attempts to deny God's agency any role in the particularities of history and nature, there are theologians who have refused to give up trying to find a place for divine actions *in* the world. While there is a general tendency to think of divine action as conforming to what Kaufman called God's master act and Maurice Wiles's notion of the world as "a single divine act"[13] rather than as a place where God acts discretely from time to time, performing acts that are uniquely God's, there are theologians who think they can find what Austin Farrer called "the causal joint" between human and divine action in the world. Farrer is suspicious of ever finding such a joint because there is no place in the world for God to act in particular ways given that "the pattern of physical forces fills all the time [and] all the space there is, and allows no irruption from the divine."[14] The most Farrer (and Thomas Tracy who draws upon Farrer in this respect) can do is appeal to something they call "double agency," which holds that an occurrence is caused *both* by God *and* the human agent (though the mechanism for this double agency and what the unique contribution of each agent is in it remains obscure).[15] Much as Bultmann did, Farrer calls upon us to accept by faith that God is somehow present in the human act. Vincent Brümmer has correctly critiqued Farrer and Wiles on this point saying that "the claim that God brings about *all* events excludes the possibility of identifying particular events as acts of God distinct from the rest which we ascribe to other agents. . . . [This claim] would seem in the end to make all talk of divine agency vacuous" because there is nothing distinctive about it and gives us no information about God's purposes or intentions.[16] If God cannot perform specific, historically distinct acts then God is not much of an agent at all.

---

13. Maurice Wiles, *God's Action in the World* (London: SCM, 1986), 29.
14. Austin Farrer, *The Freedom of the Will* (London: Adam & Charles Black, 1958), 313.
15. Austin Farrer, *Faith and Speculation*, (London: Adam & Charles Black, 1967), 159.
16. Vincent Brümmer, "Farrer, Wiles and the Causal Joint," *Modern Theology* 8, no. 1 (January 1992): 7.

God and the Quantum Level

One of the more recent and intriguing attempts to "fit" God's acts into the causal nexus is by locating God's action only at the lowest quantum level of nature, a level that is declared by many to be 'indeterminate'[17] (i.e., not completely subject to deterministic prediction). This indeterminancy applies both to our inability to conceptually predict what is going to take place at the quantum or micro level of reality and what is actually taking place at that level. In other words, indeterminancy is ontological as well as epistemological. Events at the quantum level are unpredictable, and that fact indicates (but does not prove) that the quantum world is ontologically indeterminate (not deterministically caused by macro-entities at the causal level). Physicist and theologian Robert Russell asserts that quantum processes underlie macroscopic features of the world.[18] Natural objects or entities in the macroscopic, natural, or causal world do not cause quantum events. Science cannot locate a natural cause for a quantum event. There is genuine chance or randomness at the quantum level. That is, unless something somehow "acts" to resolve the randomness in a particular way and toward a particular end. But when the indeterminacy at the quantum level is resolved by action, including divine action (in a way that no observer can see or explain given only the explanatory tools of causal law at the macroscopic level) that act eventually produces consequences at the macroscopic level. This presumably protects divine action from causal explanation while at the same time giving it some kind of efficacy in the macroscopic causal world.

In quantum theory, if God "causes" a quantum event then God's "causality" is not in competition with natural causes. Quantum divine action does not reduce God's action to the status of another natural cause if we understand indeterminism in an ontological sense. God's role in determining quantum processes is quite unlike natural causality and thus, one might argue, avoids the dreaded problem of "intervention" into the natural order. As Russell says, "It is no longer necessary to conceive of divine actions as intervening in the regular processes of nature." He believes that "without the existence of quantum chance as evidence of ontological indeterminacy 'it is hard to see how human—or divine—agency really makes sense.'"[19] This leads him to assert a "new view of special providence, which holds both that God acts in the world

---

17. I am indebted to the work of Nicholas Saunders in his *Divine Action and Modern Science* (Cambridge: Cambridge University Press, 2002) for my understanding of the attempts to use quantum theory to interpret divine action in the world.

18. Saunders, *Divine Action and Modern Science*, 110.

19. Ibid., 112.

objectively [at the quantum level] and that God does so without intervening in or suspending the laws of nature [at the macroscopic level]." This is what he means by "noninterventionist objective special divine action."[20] According to Russell, "God acts together with nature to bring about a quantum event. Nature provides the necessary causes, but God's action together with nature constitutes the sufficient cause of the occurrence of the event. . . . God acts in all quantum events, but in some cases, the effects 'matter' in the classical [macro] world more than in other cases."[21]

It is crucial to this quantum-based approach to insist that whatever God does at the quantum level must have effects at the cosmic or macro level. (Otherwise, why bother thinking of God as agent at all?) However, just how that happens without God's action at the quantum level—*intervening* in that level in some way—is not clear. It seems to be the case that quantum theologians avoid interventionist reference by insisting that intervention is what happens only at the macroscopic level (where causal law pertains exhaustively) but not "below" that level. This distinction between macro and quantum interventions is not entirely clear or well justified.

Nevertheless, appeal to action at the quantum level is another attempt to get around the problem of intervention in a closed causal nexus. But the appeal presupposes the very thing that ought to be in question: namely, that interventionism is a fundamental problem for understanding action, both divine and human. Russell believes that God's action at the quantum level is not an intervention at the macroscopic level of nature. God's acts realize "one of several potentials in the quantum system" and do not manipulate "subatomic particles as a quasi-physical force."[22]

Theologian Nancey Murphy supplements Russell's understanding of divine action at the quantum level. She, too, rejects a God-of-the-gaps theory in which God uses the gaps in the causal order to insert God's actions. Instead, she asserts that quantum indeterminacies are "ontological rather than epistemological," meaning that there are real gaps—not just gaps in our comprehension of what takes place in the world. Assumedly, God's will is then exercised by means of the "macro-effects of subatomic manipulation."[23] "The apparently random events at the quantum level all involve (but are not exhausted by) specific, intentional acts of God."[24] It's not clear, however, how

20. Ibid.
21. Ibid., 113.
22. Ibid.
23. Ibid., 115.
24. Ibid., 116.

God's "involvement" at the quantum level is different from an "intervention" into the quantum level. At either level, such involvement makes a difference to the outcome of what would have otherwise taken place without such intervention. Nevertheless, God's action at the quantum level is restricted to the extent that it preserves at the macroscopic level a world that is exhaustively subject to causal law. God, according to Murphy, does not use action at the quantum level to destabilize the macroscopic level (and thus, presumably, has no need to perform "miracles" in the traditional interventionist sense).

QUANTUM ACTION AND THE PROBLEM OF INTERVENTIONISM

Nicholas Saunders rightly sees the problem here: as he points out, an appeal to the quantum level does not, despite claims to the contrary, ultimately avoid the problem of interventionism. As he says, "it is clearly highly interventionist for God directly to manipulate the wavefunction of quantum theory."[25] It is also, according to Saunders, "unsatisfactory for God simply to cause wavefunction collapses [a feature of quantum physics] without determining their result in some sense if God is held to act in a purposeful manner. Moreover, there is considerable difficulty in making the claim that God performs measurements without also claiming that God acts interventionistically in bringing two parts of creation [the quantum and macroscopic] to interact with each other."[26] How can the metaphysical characteristics of one level permit intervention at that level but not at another level? The only answer that I can see is that quantum theorists believe that causal law does not obtain at the quantum level. And since they are in thrall to cosmic determinism at the macro level, they are left to find divine action only at the indeterminate level below that. Saunders rightly notes, however, that quantum theory is finally a deterministic theory.[27] And if intervention is what occurs when any agent acts, and if intervention is not a threat to the reliability of causal explanation even at the macro level, then intervention should not be a threat to the notion of any agent's action or to the causal order as its exists in the absence of agents acting.

Thomas Tracy adds to the support for quantum divine action by suggesting that the gaps in the world that quantum physics points to are sufficiently open to permit divine action without God intervening at the non-quantum level. These gaps in the order of nature are "'open' in ways that accommodate divine action without disruption" of the natural order.[28] The

25. Ibid., 156.
26. Ibid.
27. Ibid., 132.
28. Ibid., 121.

openness of the quantum level permits influence (but not causality or intervention) from outside the quantum level, and in such a way that there are important macroscopic events that they "effect." Tracy is also driven by a deep fear of intervention at the macroscopic or causal level. He rejects a notion of God as an agent "jostling for influence in the midst of many others on the cosmic scene."[29] But it's not clear why he would be troubled by this kind of "jostling" by God while presumably not being bothered by the way in which human agents jostle each other within the common ontological space of their actions.

Unfortunately, in the end, all quantum theorists are still in thrall to the Kantian-inspired closed causal model and find God's action only, as Tracy puts it, at the "lowest level in the substructure of God's acts. . . . in those events that lie at the bottom, as it were, of the instrumental hierarchies that achieve God's purpose in the world."[30] But why, one might ask, locate divine action only at the *bottom*? Pols's notion of an act-hierarchy locates action as originating at the *top* of the spatio-temporal elements that comprise the infrastructure through which the act manifests itself downward, as it were, pervading and unifying the whole temporal-spatial infrastructure. Finding divine action only at the quantum level abdicates the primordiality and pervasiveness of action, which controls a broad range of macro as well as microscopic elements by wielding and unifying them into a single whole known simply as the act.

Despite their failure to explain satisfactorily what is different about a divine intervention at the quantum level as opposed to an intervention at the macroscopic level, not all quantum theorists are dogmatic on this point. Tracy, as I read him, is open enough to suggest at one point, (and quite correctly I believe) that "the most we can expect . . . is to make the case that there is *some* structure of action, coherent with the rest of what we believe about the world, by which the divine agent might bring about the kinds of higher order acts that we come . . . to attribute to God."[31] This is absolutely right. I only differ from Tracy in believing that the structure of action as defined by Macmurray, Pols, and Tallis provides a better, more coherent model than one that looks only to the subatomic level for divine action. Looking only there misses the fullness of an act that pervades the whole infrastructure from the top down and not just at its subatomic level.

29. Ibid., 122.
30. Tracy, "Narrative Theology," 179.
31. Thomas F. Tracy, "Divine Action, Created Causes, and Human Freedom," in *The God Who Acts: Philosophical and Theological Explorations*, ed. Thomas F. Tracy (University Park, PA: Pennsylvania State University Press, 1994), 83

Divine Interference Without Reductionism

If one starts with the assumption that only deterministic, reductionist causal explanations are appropriate for all that occurs in the world, then, of course, reference to an agent "interfering" in the causal order would be unacceptable, whether it's a human agent or a divine one. But if we take the common sense view found in Tallis, Pols, Macmurray, Ward, and others, that actions are not simply causes in the same way that non-intentional forces are causes, then reduction of all occurrences to strictly causal explanation is not the only option.

In one sense, of course, it is perfectly natural to revert to "interference" language since actions always bring about something that would not have happened if the causal structure ran forward on its own without agent intervention. Every scientific prediction is conditioned (explicitly or implicitly) by the proviso: x will cause y "provided nothing interferes." The apple will drop from the tree when the stem is no longer able to hold it provided that someone does not pick it before that. My eyes will blink so many times a minute provided that I don't interfere with that pattern by intentionally speeding it up or slowing it down according to some purpose I have in mind. In short, I interfere in the closed causal nexus whenever I intentionally disrupt the natural or regular course of events that will occur, absent my action, in a predictable way according to the causal laws appropriate for that range of events. This kind of intervention seems unproblematic unless one assumes that there are *no* free actions at all, every occurrence being exhaustively determined by causal law.

Therefore, if we want to employ the notion of "interference," it should not be understood contrary to reason as that of an alien intruder trying to break into a causal structure that is understood in strictly reductionist C-E terms. It is an "interference," to be sure, but a perfectly normal one that happens whenever an agent deploys or utilizes the causal structure to bring about a result that the causal chain would not, of its own accord, produce (unless by some extraordinary and by definition unpredictable coincidence). To use Pols's terminology, an action is a "real causality" that *uses and deploys* the C-E relations in order to bring about the realization of the agent's intention. An agent's act is not a causal event that has to "fit into" the C-E structure. Reversing the traditional imagery, it is better to think of the C-E relation as fitting into the agent's act as the means for its realization; it is simply not helpful to try to think of the act fitting into the C-E relation as one cause among others within it.

The imagery of intervention into the causal structure would not be conceptually problematic if we could accept the argument that *all* actions (as distinct from mere happenings or events) are, in a way unique to actions, interferences into an otherwise closed causal order. It is the "otherwise" that is key. Macmurray has made a great deal out of the notion of interference, not with respect to divine action, but with respect to human action. Scientific reductionism is, in one sense, to be commended for the logical consistency of holding to the closed causal order and ultimately denying the possibility and conceivability of free human actions within it. Most action theorists, however, are inevitably drawn to some notion of interference simply in order to make sense of human free action, assuming that they do not want to equate or reduce such action to events entirely determined by non-intentional natural causes. And as William Alston, the late Christian philosopher of God and action, boldly said, "God can interfere with their [autonomous created agents] activities at any time."[32]

So we have two choices: continue to use "interventionist" language to do justice to the kind of actions that *all agents'* actions entail (and thus God's actions as well), or exploit Pols's argument that actions do not have to "fit into" the causal nexus. While I believe the "interference" model does make sense when understood without its problematic connotations, it is too laden by current misunderstanding and the hold of causal law as determinative of all occurrences, including actions, to get much of a hearing. I would prefer, therefore, to move in Pols's direction and free action from the Gordian knot of the causal model i.

Pols's argument suggests that we are looking for God's act in the wrong way and the wrong place if we assume that God's acts (and ours as well) are causes in the traditional C-E sense; that we have to "fit" God's actions into a closed causal nexus that has no room for them. The whole point of his analysis of action is that *actions are not causes* in the C-E sense but constitute a different category altogether. There is no reason not to accept the claim that C-E causation occurs *within* a closed structure in which no agent-initiated actions occur. So we embark on a futile quest if we try to fit actions into a C-E structure. But if agent-initiated actions do occur, they occur by supervening upon and then utilizing and unifying—not by fitting into—the C-E structure.

If it used to explain action, the dominance of the C-E model necessarily forces explanation of divine acts (and human acts as well) into the absurd position of having to conform to C-E laws when, in fact, the act "uses" the C-E laws to express itself. Instead, Pols is suggesting that C-E laws need to conform to or make themselves available to the unifying power of the controlling act that wields them into a unified whole.

---

32. William P. Alston, "God's Action in the World," in *Divine Nature and Human Language: Essays in Philosophical Theology* (Ithaca, NY: Cornell University Press, 1989), 204.

So how do we know that we are dealing with an action rather than with a fully caused event (no agent involved)? By observing over time whether it coheres with a series of alleged other actions to reveal a pattern, whether we can discern an overarching intention that wields each occurrence into a unity under a description as acts, or instantiations, of that intention. At one level we have no problem with determining whether another person's "doings" are acts or simply happenings (e.g., eye blinking or arm raising) occurrences that, prior to analysis, could be either pure causal happenings or intentional actions. To make the proper determination, we work, in effect, from such things as inferences, clues, evidence, traces, testimony, and after-the-fact confessions by the agent.

Basic and Indirect Actions

Human acts can be either basic or indirect. A basic action is performed simply by the agent doing it without the assistance of prior acts. I blink my eyes without first doing something else in order to get my eyes to blink. I decide to blink my eyes and they blink provided nothing prevents them from blinking. My decision to blink my eyes originates a sequence of causes and effects (e.g., neuron firings) that eventually culminate in my eyes blinking. In most cases, I am completely oblivious of the "mechanics" of how my decision initiates and controls this set of causal happenings. When I am not even thinking about blinking my eyes they blink anyway, not because I've intended them to blink but because there are immanent biological causes in the causal nexus of my body that bring about their blinking according to the regularities of nature.

Actions are always actions under a description. If the intent of my act is to get my friend's attention, then blinking at him is an indirect means by which I hope to accomplish that end. If I could perform a basic action without utilizing causal intermediaries (e.g., I just wish for his attention and it happens), then I would not need to use other indirect actions such as blinking. But if we are focusing simply on *how* I brought about the blinking, that action is direct or basic and does not pose a conceptual problem.

If God is an agent in roughly the same sense in which we are agents, then God's acts are in this sense almost always "basic" actions or, as Pols prefers to call them, "originative actions."[33] That is, they are performed directly by God: they originate in and from God as the agent whose acts then ramify in and unify a whole host of causal elements within the infrastructure that they are unifying. But God can also use God's basic acts as a means to achieve more indirectly a more inclusive or far-reaching intention. God could directly cause

---

33. Pols, *Meditation on a Prisoner*, 96.

a bush to burn without being consumed—not as an end in itself—but as a means of getting Moses' attention. The initiation of the burning is a basic act and the attention getting is an indirect act. If God is a maximal exemplification or primordial instance of what it means to be an agent, then these kinds of actions (on a far greater and more inclusive scale) are available to God just as they are, in a more limited way, to human agents.

Alston on Divine Acts

Many contemporary philosophers of religion are deeply sympathetic to the notion of God as a personal agent. William Alston has famously said that he has no trouble thinking of God as a timeless agent who produces temporal effects. "I think of God as literally a personal agent."[34] Alston accepts that what it is for God to intend something may be "radically different" from what it is for humans to intend something. Yet the "basic sense" of the term "agent" holds constant across the divine-human gap. As we noted earlier Alston has no problem with the notion of God interfering with the activities of other agents at any time. Even Tracy, who seems to find divine action only at the quantum level, has said that God is that individual in whom the capacities that define agency find their maximal expression.[35]

Alston does not directly explain *how* God performs the actions that he thinks can be literally ascribed to God. As his previous comment indicates, however, he has no problem thinking of divine actions as "interferences" with the actions of human agents and, one assumes by extension, with the causal structure of the world in which human beings act. Just because something would be "a violation of the law of nature" would not, in Alston's opinion, render such actions impossible.[36] And he asks, "Why should we assume that God would prefer to attain His goals only by working through the natural order if He could? . . . It is presumptuous for any human being to claim that degree of insight into the divine preference order."[37]

Yet, for the most part, Alston does not think we need to invoke miracles or violations of the law of nature in order to explain divine action. In a way that is remarkably consistent with Macmurray's and Pols's view of the relation between action and the causal order, Alston says that "the most we are ever justified in accepting in the way of nomologically sufficient conditions is a law

---

34. Alston, "God's Action in the World," 198.
35. Tracy, "Narrative Theology," 177.
36. Alston, "God's Action in the World," 211.
37. Ibid., 210, note 15.

[of nature] that specifies what will (must) ensue in the absence of any relevant factors other than those specified in the law . . . the laws we have adequate reason to accept lay down sufficient conditions only within a 'closed system' . . . none of the laws we are capable of working with take account of all possible influences; even if a formulation took account of all influences with which we are acquainted, we cannot be assured that there are no hitherto unknown influences lurking on the horizon."[38] At a much more mundane level, of course, all intentions are "influences lurking on the horizon" and when they are acted upon they break open what is, in the absence of those actions, an otherwise closed system.

"Since the laws we work with make (implicit or explicit) provision for interference by outside forces unanticipated by the law, it can hardly be claimed that the law will be violated if a divine outside force intervenes."[39] And I would add the same proviso applies to human actions. When I act, I do something that overrides or supervenes upon the laws of nature that, in the absence of my action, would produce a result that is completely caused by non-agential forces. This means, for Alston, that the phrase "'outside the ordinary course of nature' does not imply 'a violation of a law of nature.'"[40]

For Alston, when God brings something about intentionally God has performed a divine act. God "enters the process from time to time as an agent,"[41] but not, suggests Alston, through a body since God does not have a body. At times, despite his clear use and defense of interventionist language in other places, Alston is reluctant to speak of divine "interventions" or "interferences." Nevertheless, God does provide, according to an "action plan,"[42] a "causal input that alters how things would have gone had only natural factors been operative."[43] The problem with the term "intervention" for Alston (in his more reluctant moments) is that it suggests a deist picture of God as essentially "outside" creation. Yet, in the end, Alston keeps coming back to the language of divine intervention[44] in a way that is not alien to the Tallis-Pols-Macmurray understanding of action. He is using it in what we might call the benign, neutral, or non-problematic sense of intervention: namely, that act by which

---

38. Ibid., 212.
39. Ibid.
40. Ibid.
41. William P. Alston, "Divine Action: Shadow or Substance," in *The God Who Acts*, ed. Thomas F. Tracy (University Park, PA: Pennsylvania State University Press, 1994), 44.
42. William P. Alston, "An Action-Plan Interpretation of Purposive Explanations of Actions," in *Theory and Decision* 20, no. 3 (1986): 275.
43. Alston, "Divine Action," 45.
44. Ibid.

the agent intervenes into the causal nexus in order to bring about a result that purely natural forces (absent agential origination) would not have brought about. This, as I have argued, is a non-problematic use of intervention since it does not conflict with the notion of the deployment of the causal infrastructure by the originating act of an agent who presides over or supervenes upon that infrastructure. If we resist using the notion of intervention even for human acts, then we deprive ourselves of a way of conceptualizing the difference between acts and purely causal occurrences. How else could we describe my choosing to blink my eyes so as to distinguish it from my eyes blinking because they were caused to do so by biological/physiological forces within my body? Intervention in this case (and thousands like it) does not seek to *undermine* the usefulness of causal explanation but only to restrict it to those occurrences that have no agential intention initiating them. I would not want to abandon the notion of intervention entirely despite the misuse to which it is often put in order to suggest a radical conflict between divine acts and what takes place in the closed causal order. But if one takes that order as absolutely self-contained, then there is no place in it even for human action—let alone divine action—and that is too high a price to pay for preserving the sanctity of the causal order that, strictly interpreted in a reductionist fashion, has no room for intentional actions of any kind.

On the other hand, if the world is not a closed causal nexus of intramundane events, then actions can take place any time an agent chooses to "intervene" in that nexus. But if Pols is right, then intervention, while a perfectly legitimate way of understanding actions, simply may not be as good a term as "supervention": the apex being wielding or deploying the causal nexus from the top down (vertical causality) to instantiate an intention through an act.

Peacocke, Clayton, and the Panentheistic Option

Pols's metaphysics of action is complemented by other significant contemporary philosophers of religion who also challenge the traditional and dualistic view of action as interference into a closed chain of causally locked events. As I suggested in the preface, I find myself quite sympathetic to these philosophers who are advancing ideas of action that try to get around the problem of interference or violation of causal law by appealing to notions of "downward," top-down, or part/whole causation in which an enveloping or literally *comprehensive* entity includes within itself the levels of being that it influences without having to "break into" those levels from outside them. They find intervention an entirely unacceptable idea. For example, Arthur Peacocke has insisted that "intervention" by God into the deterministic laws of the causal order "is an incoherent idea."⁴⁵ While I think this is too extreme a claim given that a divine agent, who presumably creates such laws, must never be unable to intervene within them whether or not that divine agent ever chooses to do so. As long as agents supervene the laws they utilize, they cannot be ontologically incapable of altering them. Nevertheless, intervention into a realm of reality from outside the agent is a concept that raises more problems than it solves. Philip Clayton rightly notes that relying on the notion of intervention would seem to "threaten the integrity of [the natural order], disrupting the regularity and predictability of the natural world that is necessary for free and reasonable human action."⁴⁶ For Clayton and others, including Peacocke and Haught, a non-interventionist model relies on a panentheistic (from "pan" = all, "en" = in, "theos" = God, literally all things *in* God) understanding of the divine relation to the world. Panentheism, developed most fully by A.N. Whitehead and process philosophers, is a decidedly anti-dualist model of the metaphysical order that does not separate God from the world nor does it identify them. The world, according to Clayton, must neither be external to God or identical to God.⁴⁷ By stressing that the world is "in" God, panentheism intends to avoid ontological dualism. For panentheism, a theory of divine agency no longer confronts the problem of absolute differentness,⁴⁸ a problem that we saw earlier bedevils extreme forms of dualism. The notion of downward causation proposed by the panentheists has the virtue of locating action "within" the agent rather than as an irruption of an otherwise closed causal order "outside" the agent into which the agent is seeking to insert his or her actions. Downward causation as Clayton defines it is "the process whereby some whole has an active non-additive causal influence on its parts."⁴⁹ Or, as Peacocke notes, the notion of divine creation on the panentheistic model is one in which one must say, paradoxically, that God creates a world that is other than Godself but creates it "within" (!) Godself.⁵⁰ God is conceived, in Peacocke's words, as the "unifying, unitive source and centered influence on the world's activity . . . as exerting

---

45. Arthur Peacocke, "God's Interaction with the World," in *Chaos and Complexity: Scientific Perspectives on Divine Action*, ed. Robert John Russell, Nancey Murphy, and Arthur Peacocke (Berkeley, CA: Vatican Observatory and The Center for Theology and the Natural Sciences, 1997), 278 n. 34.
46. Philip Clayton, *The Problem of God in Modern Thought* (Grand Rapids, MI: Eerdmans, 2000), 504.
47. Ibid., 505.
48. Ibid.
49. Philip Clayton, *Mind and Emergence: From Quantum to Consciousness* (Oxford: Oxford University Press, 2004), 49–50.
50. Arthur Peacocke, *Creation and the World of Science* (Oxford: Clarendon, 1979), 142.

continuously top-down causative influences on the world-as-a-whole in a way analogous to that whereby we in our thinking can exert effects on our bodies in a 'top-down' manner."[51] This approach also uses the concept, common to Pols, of "supervening" action. Peacocke says that God interacts with the world at a "supervenient" level of totality but without contravening the natural laws.[52]

This panentheistic approach has much to recommend it and in previous works I've shown my sympathy toward a process model. Nevertheless, I see it as complementary—not identical—to the approach set forth by Macmurray and Pols.

My abiding qualm about the panentheistic approach (which is similar to my qualm about Pols's Being Absolute idea) is its hesitancy to identify God as a singular Being capable of acts that are uniquely God's, opting instead for the notion of God as that reality in which all actions are contained; a reality in which divine agency, according to Clayton, "is a matter of causal sequences that are internal to God."[53] I believe the Pols approach does a bit more toward maintaining a suitable ontological distance between God and the beings upon which God acts in a supervenient way but without separating them from each other to the extent that dualism does. On the panentheistic model, it is not clear what constitutes "otherness" and how it is compatible with being "in" the creator.

The difference between Pols's notion of the Apex Being and the panentheistic notion of God as the singular whole within which all other beings are nested or contained may seem trivial. But in my rendering of the Apex Being in comparison with panentheism, beings don't have to be "in" God to be infused with God's power so that they can also act. The action-based relational model is somewhat more persuasive to me than the participatory model because there must be some ontological space between the beings that are in relation. Otherwise one moves toward Meister Eckhart's undifferentiated oneness or monist model. And Clayton, for example, is not shy about embracing the concept of monism for his panentheistic view.[54]

Pols on Participatory Power

What links Pols's view and that of the panentheists is the notion of participatory power. For Pols, Being Absolute is compresent with all the finite agents and

---

51. Arthur Peacocke, *Theology for a Scientific Age* (Oxford: Basil Blackwell, 1990), 161.
52. Peacocke, *Theology for a Scientific Age*, 159.
53. Clayton, *The Problem of God in Modern Thought*, 505.
54. Clayton, *Mind and Emergence*, 54, 198.

makes possible their action in the world. Thus, "if there are particular primary beings that exercise power in action, then they do so by virtue of their status as participant powers. . . ." The "primary being or one of its acts is the bearer of a Being that transcends it." [55] Pols admits a certain "ontological mystery" here: it is the mystery of the "concrete particular whose very particularity includes a union with and dependence upon a general, common, or universal power."[56] The individual or fundamental (finite) agent, Pols insists, "comes out of Being." The Being's unity, power, and order is a "shared one: it participates in, [and] is a partial expression of, the unity of Being."[57] Each fundamental being is a 'power instance' of a common One." [58] This One or Being, for Pols, is God. It is *a* "One whose power ramifies in all multiplicities."[59] God is the U-factor in our experience, that which transcends each of the particulars that participate in it.[60] Both Pols and panentheists want to tie the actions of finite agents to the power of Being resident in the power of Being itself.

Yet, as I suggested in my earlier critique of Pols, while this panentheistic approach (and Pols's as well) seeks to avoid metaphysical dualism, it runs the risk of veering toward a form of monism that might be better avoided if we stick to the primordiality of action emanating from distinct agents, each of whom maintains some kind of ontological space of its own and not from agents who are themselves nested within God. The panentheist approach is a little too close for comfort to a view in which the unique ontological status of agents, including that of God, is threatened by a oneness that is overly monistic.

I confess, nonetheless, that the differences between holistic, even monist, panentheism and my own approach fade into insignificance when compared with their mutual rejection of dualism and mutual embrace of action as a basic category for understanding both human and divine agency.

In general, as I have argued, this is the virtue of Macmurray's and Pols's notion of action as primordial and supervening the causal order, a supervention that includes rather than excludes the causal order in which non-agent originated events occur. So the only difference, in the end, between the approach of Pols-Macmurray and that of the panentheists is one regarding which metaphysical model or metaphor best captures the primordiality of action. But what is clear from all these approaches is the common rejection of

---

55. Pols, "The Ontology of the Rational Agent," *Review of Metaphysics* 33, no. 4 (June 1980): 709.
56. Pols, *Meditation on a Prisoner*, 332.
57. Ibid., 319.
58. Ibid., 332.
59. Ibid., 327.
60. Edward Pols, *Mind Regained* (Ithaca, NY: Cornell University Press, 1998), 119.

ontological dualism and the tacit acceptance of the notion of "intervention" by action into the causal order if intentional action is understood to be different from pure causality. The question is whether some form of monism (such as panentheism) is the only logical alternative to dualism. I think there is a middle ground, namely the primordiality of action, in which the unique status of agents is preserved without threatening to collapse into the oneness of a monist view.

6

Theology and the Discernment of God's Acts in History

From Metaphysics to Theology

So far, I have tried to lay out an essentially philosophical or metaphysical case for understanding God through the primordiality of the concept of action or agency. I have tried to show how such a concept can comprehend God acting in the world without either "violating" the laws of cause and effect or being subsumed under them. But the question remains: if God is an agent, and if God has exercised agency by acting in the world, how do we discern what those actions are? In other words, how are they picked out from all the other acts that constitute history? As we pursue this question, we move from strictly philosophical analysis into the work of theology, which attempts to identify from within the faith perspective of a particular religious tradition the central acts of God in history. Whether it is possible to identify divine acts outside the theological perspective is a question we will need to consider.

Despite resistance from many of its practitioners, theology presumes a metaphysical basis for the notion of God. The work of theology is meaningless unless it presupposes that God acts in the world and expects a response to those acts. But the assumption that God acts implies a metaphysical view of God as an agent, that is, it assumes that God is a particular kind of entity, an agent, not a rock. In this chapter, I want to explore the intersection between the metaphysics of agency and theology's attempt to identify specific kerygmatic divine acts, despite the fact that some contemporary theologians, such as Kevin Hector in his *Theology Without Metaphysics*, believe that there can be a theology without metaphysics. Hector's view is a continuation of the rejection of "natural theology" grounded in the dogmatic theology of Karl Barth who believed that philosophy must not intrude on or set the conditions for the unique revelation of God in the Christ event, a revelation he claimed was not available to philosophy working independently of theology. But Barth's and Hector's hesitancy to accept a metaphysical view of God as agent overlooks the fact that any reference to a divine revelation—no matter how it is positioned alongside of or in conflict with "natural" events—already presupposes at least a minimal commitment to the metaphysical view that God is of such a nature as to be able to act through God's revelations in a world that is other than Godself. The argument I have pursued so far in developing the primordiality of the concept of agency for God is not at odds with the theological project of specifying divine acts in history. My analysis can, however, be supplemented and expanded by bringing it into conversation with some selected contemporary systematic theologians in the Christian tradition whose work complements that of the philosophers I have drawn upon in advancing my project of understanding God as agent. I will take up the issue of metaphysics more fully in my discussion of the work of theologian Wolfhart Pannenberg later in this chapter.

COMMON GROUND FOR THEOLOGY AND PHILOSOPHY

As I have tried to argue, there is a philosophically persuasive case for affirming the primordiality of agency. And that case, which corresponds to the implicit metaphysical assumptions of theology (even when they sometimes seem to be hidden from theologians), requires us to make some assumptions common to both philosophy and theology.

One, that the conception of a divine agent is not self-contradictory or inappropriate for a divine reality "worthy of worship," and this I hope to have shown in the earlier chapters of this book. Two, that if God is an agent capable of performing historical actions in the space-time continuum alongside other agents, then divine acts are not so radically or ontologically different from human acts as to be incapable of being conceived in roughly the same way in which we conceive human acts. Again, this I believe I have shown in my arguments so far in the book. There must be some univocity to the notion of "act" that captures both divine actions and human actions. (This univocal sense of action does not, of course, rule out enormous differences between divine and human acts with respect to the magnitude of their power, efficacy, range, moral quality, decisiveness, etc.) But if they are completely ontologically different, we will have gotten nowhere in relating divine and human action.

Three, that God can perform "discrete" or particular acts in history. God need not be the author who has performed only a single "master act" (i.e., the sweep of history in its entirety, a kind of pre-temporal "act" that does not touch down in history at any particular times and places). If God is an agent, then God can be the creator of the whole space-time infrastructure but also the author of particular acts for which God is *uniquely* responsible within that infrastructure.

Theology carries out the task of discerning which specific acts are divinely originated.

If God can be conceived in a metaphysically respectable way as an agent, it would seem to follow that God would have left enough evidence of divine actions in the world to permit a reasonable inference to both God's existence as agent and to the divine character (since character is always inferred from and revealed through an agent's actions). And yet many theologians in the western tradition have been loathe to base a knowledge of God primarily, let alone exclusively, on a reading of God's alleged historical actions apart from or independent of a theological perspective. Purportedly divine actions have seemed to be a less than reliable basis on which to build a belief about who God is and what God is up to. As G.E. Lessing once said, "the accidental truths of history can never become the proof of the necessary truths of reason."[1] If philosophy gives us the conceptual tools for understanding the metaphysical possibility of divine action grounded in a divine agent, then history as it is discerned through the work of theology gives us a basis for claiming to know the *meaning* of divine action. Philosophy gives us the metaphysical basis for claiming a conception of God as agent; theology gives us the basis for discerning where that divine agent has actually acted. This mutual work of philosophy and theology has even led John Macmurray to see them as very closely related—at least in outcome, if not in method.

MACMURRAY ON THEOLOGY

Macmurray believes that we must, if we are being fully rational, see the world in its totality as God's action (not discounting the possibility of specific divine acts within the world). If our primordial category of understanding is the agent, the world in its totality must be conceived as the field of action for the supreme or apex agent (where else would God act?). And this means that the world is, as Macmurray puts it, God's act: God is the universal "Other" from which the community of persons distinguishes itself. But only personal agents can be in personal relationships with each other, and therefore we must conceive God as the personal Other with whom we stand in relation. "I must determine myself and the Other reciprocally, by means of the same categories.... Consequently I must characterize the Other in the same terms, as an Agent acting intentionally

---

1. G.E. Lessing, "On the Proof of the Spirit and of Power," in *Lessing's Theological Writings*, ed. and trans. Henry Chadwick (Stanford, CA: Stanford University Press, 1956), 53, 55. But this gets the argument backwards: if one starts with the ontological or metaphysical primordiality of agency, then one looks to history in order to discern whether there are historical acts that reveal the intentions and actions of the agents who performed them, including those of God, the supreme personal agent.

in relation to me."² This is a metaphysically based conception of God, and it is validated or "proved" only when we act upon it, when we assume its reality in practice. And so, according to Macmurray, in language that would be equally at home in theology and philosophy, "we relate ourselves rightly to the world by entering into communion with God, and seeking to understand and to fulfill his intention."³ "We must think the world as one action . . . to conceive it as the act of God,⁴ the Creator of the world, and ourselves as created agents, with a limited and dependent freedom to determine the future, which can be realized only on the condition that our intentions are in harmony with His intention, and which must frustrate itself if they are not."⁵

---

2. John Macmurray, *Persons in Relation* ,Introduction by Frank G. Kirkpatrick. New York: Humanities Press, 1991), 221. This is the second volume of his Gifford Lectures of 1953–54, the first volume being *The Self as Agent* (London: Faber & Faber, 1957). Macmurray explicitly distinguishes his view from that which sees the world as a single biological evolutionary "process." A process theology does not, in Macmurray's view, proceed on the basis of the primacy of agency and thus will be one in which the status of the agent is questionable. "Events" that occur in a biological or organic process are not the same as "acts," which occur only when agents perform them.

3. Ibid., 217.

4. This need not mean that God performs only this one action, however. It should be taken to mean that God's initial act is the creation of the world but that subsequent to that act God may perform numerous other discrete actions within the world God has created. See also Macmurray's final chapter "The World as One Action" in *The Self as Agent*, in which he develops the idea that "the only way in which we can conceive our experience as a whole is by thinking the world as one action" (204). This conception, he claims, ultimately leads to a notion of the ideal of historical understanding as the representation of the "whole human past as if it were the 'memory-content' of a single agent [God] who had experienced it" (211).

5. Macmurray, *Persons in Relation*, 222. Macmurray's claim that in the long run historical experience will validate the faith or trust that only those human intentions that conform to the divine intention will be realized was developed in an earlier book called *The Clue to History* (London: Student Christian Movement Press, 1938). In order for God's intention for humankind to be realized it must "be brought to consciousness in man" (54). And, for Macmurray, this occurred in the religion of the Hebrew people and came to full consciousness in Jesus, who "marks the point in history at which it becomes possible for man to adopt consciously as his own purpose the purpose which is already inherent in his own nature" (55). Acknowledging that the coming to consciousness of God's true intentions takes a long time and multiple divergences from the path, Macmurray nonetheless holds that if God made us, then God built into our very nature the reality that we cannot be fully ourselves (i.e., fully personal and communal) unless we act in accord with who we were made to be. It should be noted, however, that in developing his argument in *The Clue to History*, Macmurray focuses (as does systematic theology) upon the work of Jesus. This suggests that the gap between Macmurray's philosophical approach developed in the Gifford Lectures and a theological approach is not nearly as wide as one might initially suspect.

THOMAS TORRANCE ON SCIENCE AND THEOLOGY

This linkage of theology and philosophy, represented by modern science, anticipates and essentially agrees with the ideas of another theologian standing in the Barthian tradition, Thomas Torrance. Much of Torrance's work is an attempt to relate what he calls scientific theology to non-reductionist science. Both "sciences" are about real (though different) objects and both require a realistic (i.e. objective) conception of their objects if our relationship to them is to be fulfilling. Torrance even cites Macmurray on this point. He notes approvingly that Macmurray holds that "we know truly and rationally only when we know objectively and . . . that it this objectivity subsisting between our personal relations that is the 'core of rationality.'"[6] But if our knowledge is real (not illusory), then we must be able to act upon it in a way that brings ultimate fulfillment of our intentions. This can only happen if our actions are performed with our intention to conform our way of life to God's intentions since the divine intentions decisively influence the final outcome of history. This decisive influence is not without suitable alterations due to human freedom of action. God's "vulnerability" and not predetermined responsiveness to human action is part of the dynamic of the relationship between personal agents, both divine and human. The performance of human actions under the guidance of an overarching divine intention then becomes a way of life.

For Christian theology the discernment of divine acts is found in the biblical narrative, which is itself grounded on the claim that it is the Word of God reflecting God's Word incarnated in Jesus. The presumption of an acting God is clearly at the heart of the biblical tradition. The Bible makes no sense unless one accepts the reality of an acting God. A God who, in some specifiable sense, does *not* act in history (i.e., does not makes God's power or presence known *in* the fabric of space-time, in addition to creating the totality of space-time as God's signature action) is a God with whom one could have no interaction and therefore no real relationship. Unless God is a "personal Someone" whose acts make a difference to the success of one's intentions in the same field of action (i.e., the created order), God's relevance for one's life would be negligible.

WALTER BRUEGGEMANN

This has certainly been true in the biblical traditions of Judaism and Christianity, which are central resources in the work of theology. As biblical scholar Walter Brueggemann said, "The characteristic claim of Israel's

---

6. Thomas Torrance, *God and Rationality* (New York: Oxford University Press, 1971), 81.

testimony is that Yahweh is an active agent who is the subject of an active verb, and so the testimony is that Yahweh, the God of Israel, has acted in decisive and transformative ways."[7] Torrance echoes this claim when he says that "the Bible without the living, acting, revealing, judging, reconciling God becomes merely an 'academic' concern of the historical and linguistic scholar."[8]

Brueggemann also acknowledges in opposition to the non-metaphysical emphasis of some theologians, that the Old Testament has an ontology that features the centrality of God as an agent. And an ontology presumes a metaphysics of the kind of beings that exist. The ontology of the biblical God is discerned from the testimony of the biblical writers regarding what they took to be their encounter with God. "After testimony the Old Testament provides a rich statement on ontology."[9] Nevertheless, Brueggemann admits that modernist or classical views of God have little place for the ontology of a divine agent. It is precisely the attempt to develop such a place through the ontology of the primordiality of agency developed by Macmurray, Raymond Tallis, and Edward Pols to whom this book is dedicated.

THE BIBLE AS THE NARRATIVE OF DIVINE ACTS IN HISTORY

For believers, the Bible becomes the story of God's acts in history. But before the specificity of theology's discernment of divine acts can make its entrance, we have the right to ask whether the way of life it commends as most fully conforming to the divine intention (e.g., self-sacrifice, compassion, justice, forgiveness, reconciliation, and nonviolence) can prove itself to someone *outside* the theological tradition, as more fulfilling than alternative ways of life (e.g., aggressive power exercised over others for the self-interest of the power wielder). Must one rely solely on theology's interpretation of the biblical narrative as the *only way* to discern God's intentions through the divine acts in history? The possibility of an extra-theological discernment cannot, it seems to me, be ruled out a priori. If it is the case that God created the world in such a way that only actions or ways of life that conform to God's real intentions can and will be realized (because God set up the world in this way), then, at least in theory, the non-theologically informed person might be able to discern what the divine intentions are and what way of life best conforms to them.

But what might be possible in theory may be impossible in practice given the sinful condition of human persons and their inevitably limited life

---

7. Walter Brueggemann, *Theology of the Old Testament* (Minneapolis: Fortress Press, 1997), 123.

8. Thomas Torrance, *Space, Time and Resurrection* (Grand Rapids, MI: Eerdmans, 1976), 3.

9. Brueggemann, *Theology of the Old Testament*, 118.

view. How does one get to the discernment that *this* way of life is both divinely created, enacted, and compelling to persons caught in a world in which contrary intentions and ways of life seem to prevail in the short run and in which human insight is clouded and distorted by human sin? This is where theology indispensably supplements the philosophical understanding of reality.

Macmurray, as we have seen, believes that philosophy can lead us to the view of God as the personal agent who unifies all of reality. He argues that by shifting our starting point for understanding reality to the primordiality of the agent's "I do" from the primacy of the thinker's "I think," we "are driven to conceive a personal universe in which God is the ultimate reality. This transformation restores its whole substance to philosophy, which again becomes the intellectual aspect of the search for the real. The problematic of philosophy lies then in the distinction between 'real' and 'unreal'" and this, he claims, "is the problematic of religious reflection; and philosophy, if it is concerned with the intellectual aspect of this problematic, must be identical with theology, with an undogmatic theology which, like science, has abandoned certainty, and which has recognized that religious doctrines, too, are all hypothetical. Philosophy, we must conclude, is theology which has abandoned dogmatism, and has become in a new and wider sense a natural theology."[10]

This reference to natural theology conforms to the mandate of the Gifford Lectures, under whose auspices Macmurray gave the lectures in 1953–54 and which were published as *The Self as Agent* and *Persons in Relation*. The lectures were established by Adam Lord Gifford, who was convinced that a natural knowledge of God would lead to human well-being and fulfillment, just as Macmurray was convinced that a philosophically grounded knowledge of God as agent would lead to a reading of human experience and history that only a way of life in harmony with God's intentions could ultimately "succeed." Gifford felt, and Macmurray agreed, that the lectures he supported would deal with the topic of natural religion "without reference to or reliance upon any supposed special exceptional or so-called miraculous revelation."[11] Gifford, I believe, misconstrued the nature of divine action by assuming an ontological difference between miracle and action. But in the ontology of action that I've developed, no such ontological difference is needed. For Macmurray, once that difference is eliminated, natural theology then becomes the basis for claiming that God can act in history. Systematic theology concentrates on which acts are divinely authored and point most persuasively to the divine intentions determining them.

10. Macmurray, *Persons in Relation*, 224.
11. For the history of the Gifford Lectures, visit http://www.giffordlectures.org/online.asp.

In principle, both philosophy and theology are capable of looking to history to find evidence of God's actions. Philosophy looks there because a supreme agent will have to manifest its intentions in history and theology looks there because it believes that God has chosen to manifest those intentions in certain particular revelatory or kerygmatic actions, which it claims to discern under the guidance of God's own spirit in interpreting the biblical narrative. Philosophy can postulate the rationality and coherence of the idea of God acting in history: theology identifies certain acts as those for which God is uniquely responsible and that decisively determine the course of history. The centrality of history for a theological understanding of God's revelations is explored more fully in the work of Wolfhart Pannenberg further on in this chapter.

ALVIN PLANTINGA

But even Christian thinkers do not universally accept the importance of history in our knowledge of God. Christian philosopher Alvin Plantinga, who is committed to the truth of the "central" Biblical claims about who God is and what God is up to and supports a contemporary form of natural theology, is reluctant to rely exclusively upon historical evidence for knowing God's existence and nature. His reluctance is due to his attempt to make Christian belief properly basic, that is, without need of evidential or inferential support.[12] He not only thinks historical inference is not strong enough to warrant belief in God, but he is also convinced that through the direct action of God upon the believer's consciousness (which, however, is a form of divine action), the truth about God is given to and sealed cognitively in the mind of the believer.

But there is a certain oddity in this reluctance to base a belief about a God who acts on a discernment of what one takes to be God's historical actions. If God is truly an agent with unlimited powers in utilizing the causal infrastructure of the world, and does act in history, then surely one would expect that a series of divine actions that formed the core of a witness to their efficaciousness in creating a people (Israel) and bringing about two religious traditions (Judaism and Christianity) would be accessible for interpretation by all human beings even without being participants in those faith traditions. All these alleged acts of God were of a public nature: available for interpretation by anyone. A God who acts and whose acts decisively change the course of

---

12. "I don't *need* a good historical case for the truth of the central teachings of Gospel to be warranted in accepting them.... the warrant for Christian belief doesn't require that I or anyone else have this kind of historical information ... It doesn't require to be validated or proved by some source of belief *other* than faith, such as historical investigation." Alvin Plantinga, *Warranted Christian Belief* (New York: Oxford University Press, 2000), 259.

history forever but who can't be known through those acts is a peculiar God and so is an epistemological situation in which knowledge of God through God's own acts is impossible or at least profoundly difficult. If knowledge of God based on God's historical acts is *completely* dependent on a faith-based interpretive framework not available to those outside it, one would have to wonder why God couldn't or didn't make Godself known more publicly, albeit also elusively. It is almost as if, no matter how hard he tries, God can't make Godself known through the record of God's acts in history unless we first have recourse to a Plantinga type knowledge that appears to be indifferent to historical investigation.

ACTING ON BELIEFS ABOUT DIVINE ACTS IN HISTORY

If acts are the evidence through which we know the existence and character of the agents who perform them, then at some point the beliefs I form about them on the basis of the evidential trail will have to be tested and validated in and through my ongoing interaction with and response to the agents who performed them. My beliefs must prove reliable not just in meeting standards of doxastic practice but also in successfully informing my future behavior. Inferences drawn from history, however, don't have the same kind of certainty that comes with properly basic beliefs or with analytic truths. As beliefs derived *from history*, they are to be confirmed in the continuing relationships I have with the objects or persons about whom they are beliefs. This is a conclusion both theology and an appropriate philosophy can agree upon: as Macmurray puts it, "religious doctrines are as problematic as scientific theories and require like them a constant revision and a continual verification in action . . . verified only by persons who are prepared to commit themselves intentionally to the way of life they prescribe."[13]

Whether one can find acts of God apart from a theological interpretation still remains unresolved. But in the end, theology does at least give a road map for those willing to risk using it through the multiple acts that constitute history as we seek evidence of where God has been at work in the world. It enables us to see that work in a certain light and its validation of that seeing is the same as that envisioned by philosophy: the living of a way of life that proves ultimately satisfying because it conforms to God's intentions.

---

13. Macmurray, *Persons in Relation*, 223.

Divine Revelation

Part of a knowledge of God's acts in history would have to come through what those acts reveal about God's intentions. This should be the basis for saying that we know God by revelation. But this is not the revelation often appealed to when the limits of rationality have been reached. While revelation is claimed to be not in conflict with reason, in most Christian theologies it is generally given a unique epistemological status not established by reason. But, if God is an agent who acts in history, why should it require a *special* sense of revelation beyond that used in our knowledge of *any* agent's action, to discern certain acts as being of divine origin? Any act performed by an agent is a revelation of that agent's intention and thus of his or her character.[14] The ability to reveal oneself is a core part of being an agent. Torrance puts it this way: human persons have the "capacity to reveal themselves without which they may not really be known. How much truer is that of God!"[15] No ontologically other mode of revelation than that available to all agents is required for God's disclosure of the divine intentions and character.

Religious Experience

The other major source of our knowledge of God, religious experience, also implicitly entails a commitment to the notion that God acts in history. But it does not lead logically to any notion of God acting in the larger arena of history as a whole beyond the individual's immediate experience. No notion of God as the author of public "mighty acts" follows necessarily from a personal experience of divine action in one's own life. To move to the broader area of inferential knowledge from history as a whole requires one to step into an explanatory narrative more sweeping and inclusive than the experiences of one's own life even though one's own experience must "hook up" or mesh with that larger narrative in some way. Such broader narratives constitute the "background" for interpreting personal religious experience but they are not deducible from that experience, per se.

So we return to the original question: if God is an agent, then why would not the normal ways in which people come to believe in the existence (and character) of other agents also provide a basis for belief in God independent of what has traditionally been understood through theology and personal religious experience?

---

14. This statement does not, however, deny that agents can conceal their "real" intentions and personality by acting "out of character." But the very possibility of deception is grounded in the fact that actions do generally reveal what the agent is up to and what he or she is really like.

15. Torrance, *Space, Time and Resurrection*, 173.

INFERENCE TO DIVINE ACTIONS

If God does perform specific acts in history, then it would seem possible in principle to make a reasonable inference from what one takes to be some historical actions that they are the acts of God and not just the acts of other human beings—if those divine acts meet certain specifications. Assuming that one does not literally see the agent doing something, one begins with the observation of or testimony to an occurrence (or a series of occurrences) that seems to bear the marks of an action rather than a natural event (i.e., one caused solely by natural causal forces). When the ground shakes or the wind blows hard enough to dislodge loose rocks, we normally do not take the resulting configuration of the dislodged rocks to be the sign of an intentional act by an agent. On the other hand, if we find a series of rocks piled up in a repeated symmetrical fashion roughly an equal distance from each other along a path, we justifiably believe that an agent (or series of agents) produced them in accordance with a common unifying intention (i.e., we interpret them as cairns designed to mark a trail). In short, we have rough and ready criteria for making an inference that a series of "events" was either agent caused or simply "happened" as a result of purely natural causal forces. (Compare this with the classic case of my arm rising because of an unconscious neurophysical stimulus versus my arm rising because I intentionally chose to raise it. One has to dig below the appearance of the occurrence in order to determine whether it was a natural event or an agent-caused act.)

In the case of events whose precise status (acts or natural events) is unclear on the basis of direct observation alone, we are forced to look for clues as to the nature of the power that produced them. The shape and regularity of the cairns clearly indicate intentionality and thus agent origin. The scattered rocks do not. Now, if God has acted in history, one would expect some occurrences accessible to human inspection to indicate that their origin lies in a divine intention. A God who can act and does act and fails to leave enough evidence of God's actions is a strange God indeed, as would be the epistemological quandary it would put theists in. At this point, theology can provide an interpretation that makes sense of these inferred actions. Christians believe that Scripture does contain repeated testimonies to a series of occurrences construed as divine acts that constitute the history of Israel, the life and resurrection of Jesus, and the formation of the Christian church. Is the testimony to these alleged divine acts similar to the kind of witness to the acts of non-divine agents? Does theology provide a singular or unique entry into divine acts not available to the person who stands outside the faith tradition? One might argue that the problem with the biblical testimony to occurrences believed to be acts of God is that they are not supported by the kind of historical evidence most historians demand. It is important to note that the problem does not lie in the *nature* of the events reported as divine in origin. A divine agent can perform any action it chooses and, as we argued previously, all actions are interventions in (in the sense defined earlier), superventions over, or deployments of an *otherwise* closed causal nexus. This notion of action was presented in our analysis of Pols's work. A divine act is no more problematic than a human act since both are interventions or superventions in this sense.

THE CREDIBILITY OF SCRIPTURE

So it is not the nature of the act itself that it is in question (contra Lessing, Gilkey, Kaufman, et. al.) but the credibility of the historical witness to it. Today there is debate among biblical scholars as to the historical accuracy of the story of the Hebrew peoples' slavery in Egypt, their settlement of the land of Canaan, and their claims to the unique importance of Jerusalem in the tribal conflicts of that era. At the very least, the biblical witness, qualified as it is by an overlay of religious interpretation, is not sufficient to ground a well-justified claim to an inference that God is the author of the alleged acts recounted in the biblical stories. In addition, there are many acts attributed to God that hardly seem in keeping with the characterization of God as loving and peace seeking (e.g., God's commanding the slaughter of women and children, divine direct actions in causing the death of Egyptian children, etc.).

Assuming this is true, where does this leave persons who believe, for rational as distinct from theological reasons, that God has acted in history? What basis do they have for discerning divine actions in history? Must they admit that there are no alleged acts they can reference as sufficiently grounding their belief that God was their author? (They could, of course, admit that no record to date is sufficiently credible to permit them to know with certainty where and when these divine acts occurred. This admission would seriously undermine any basis for inferring God's existence from the so-called "mighty acts of God" as found in the biblical narratives.)

This may be an extreme position. The debate among biblical scholars is not settled and there are many who believe that independent research does confirm a lot of the biblical narrative, at least with respect to the actual *occurrence* of many of the events it narrates. This kind of research, of course, cannot by itself determine whether these occurrences were, in fact, divine acts. In this case, it might be possible to draw a tentative inference (always subject to subsequent correction) that God's actions as depicted in the Bible provide the *best explanation* of a series of seminal events unified under a single overarching intention. I would suggest that such an inference is not unwarranted but hardly conclusive. If it should turn out that archeology, for example, demonstrates beyond reasonable doubt that none of the events described in the Bible from the time of Abraham to the emergence of the Davidic Kingdom happened anything like the way the Bible describes them, the historical basis for believing that these events were at least partially brought about by God's direct activity would dissolve. At that point, one would either have to find an alternative and more credible testimony to the work of God in history, or one would have to resort to either religious experience alone or a natural theological argument for God that would not, as we indicated, necessarily yield the knowledge that God acts in history, let alone which specific acts God has performed.

But perhaps there is a residuum of facticity in the Biblical narrative. Perhaps after all the sifting and elimination of clearly fanciful stories and alleged events, there is some historical substratum that remains intact. For the sake of argument, let's say that this includes something like the enslavement in Egypt of a tribe of people who are later able to escape slavery and who, over time, conquer the land of Canaan. Their journey is marked by the emergence of significant leaders (such as Moses and Elijah) who transmit to them a "covenant" they believe to have come from God. They subsequently are removed from the land by occupying forces and eventually return to the land after years of exile. Later, according to Christians, one member of this tribe has a decisive impact on a small group both within and outside the tribe and is eventually declared not only to have been a miracle worker and inspiring teacher but also to have been raised from the dead. Still later, some in this group believe God has directly acted upon them in what they take to be God's bestowal of the Holy Spirit. Empowered, they then go out and create numerous communities to testify to what they think God has done and to maintain a lively witness to it. Certainly the latter occurrences are more likely to be validated by historical research than the former, according to new schools of biblical scholarship. The claims, for example, that Jesus was bodily resurrected from the dead can draw on such historical evidence as non-Christian corroboratory reference that there was a Jesus (Josephus); he was crucified; his body has never been found; there were multiple witnesses to his bodily appearance to his followers after his death; archeological and epistolary evidence of early Christian churches and their teachings, and so on. Now if one stands within the master theological narrative formed by these purported acts of God, the overall history makes sense. There is a "best explanation" for it, namely that God has been at work in the world manifesting and furthering a divine intention. The nature of that intention is itself, of course, inferred from the acts that manifest it. Traditionally, the divine intention has been interpreted as the creation of a universal, inclusive community of persons living together in bonds of justice, love, and peace (i.e., the kingdom of God on earth). This interpretation is not incoherent as it conforms to traditional religious interpretations of what God has been and is up to in the world, and it rests on *some* credible, though surely not decisive or dispositive records.

Karl Barth

At this critical juncture, we now must return to a more fully developed and more robust theology. Historic Christian theology insists that we can answer the philosophical problems we have created for ourselves only from within a perspective that believes that God has revealed God's intentions to those whose knowledge of them comes through faith. We cannot, it is claimed, work our way through the scholarly thickets we have planted without the assistance of God. Karl Barth, and many who follow in his footsteps, have forcefully claimed that unless God has chosen at God's own initiative to disclose who God is and what God is to us, we have no basis for a knowledge of God based solely on general inferences from history or nature. Our sinful condition and finite human epistemological powers make human knowledge of God impossible apart from a divine revelation, which can neither be controlled by nor comprehended in "normal" human ways of knowing. In the theological perspective of Barth, the crucial divine revelations are the incarnation and resurrection of Jesus. God enters into time and space (in Barth's view an entry incomprehensible to the human intellect given the radical discontinuity between scientific and theological understandings of time and space) and then overcomes death in and through the resurrection of God's incarnate Son. But this can be known only through God's act, not through our normal cognitive abilities. Theology, Barth insists, starts from the reality of God, "complete and whole in itself apart from and prior to the knowing activity of human individuals."[16] God "cannot be known by the powers of human knowledge, but is apprehensible and apprehended solely because of His own freedom, decision and action." What we can know by natural human intellect is at best a supreme being, but such a being "has nothing to do with God. . . . Man is able to think this being; but he has not thereby thought God. . . . Knowledge of God is not a possibility which is open for discussion. Knowledge of God takes place where

---

16. Bruce L. McCormack, *Karl Barth's Critically Realistic Dialectical Theology* (Oxford: Clarendon, 1995), 129. See also Daniel W. Hardy, "Karl Barth," in *The Modern Theologians*, ed. David E. Ford (Malden, MA: Blackwell, 2005), 24.

there is actual experience that God speaks, that He so represent Himself to man that he cannot fail to see and hear Him."[17] God is the "Wholly Other."

It is in the Christ event alone that "history is actualized, in such a way as to be accessible through participatory, personal knowledge, but *beyond access by historical investigation.*"[18] Barth assumes an "infinite qualitative distinction" between God and human beings, but this is, I believe, less an ontological or metaphysical claim (given Barth's skepticism regarding metaphysics) than it is a claim about the sinfulness of humanity that necessarily infects and distorts any "natural" knowledge we may claim to have of God. It is a claim about the radical (if not ontological) difference between God's power and holiness and our limited power and sinfulness. Barth wants to insist that whatever knowledge we have of God must be provided at God's initiative—not ours. Whoever receives the revelation of God is privileged to know God through divine grace, but it seems that apart from that grace it is impossible to know God's intentions through an "objective" reading of historical acts. Barth, therefore, implicitly answers the question, "What about those who are not privileged to receive this revelation?" They seem to be left in profound ignorance of God and God's intentions. He seems to be ruling out the possibility that a non-Christian can "read" history in such a way as to conclude that the Christian-endorsed way of life is the only one that can be ultimately satisfying. I'm not convinced that Barth's dogmatic exclusion of a non-biblical access to the divine intention is correct. I also think he draws, in his fear of metaphysics, upon a false dichotomy between God and the world even while he is presuming an unarticulated metaphysics of God as the one who acts. Nevertheless, while leaving open the logical possibility of discerning God's intentions without the benefit of the Christian faith, it may be the case that in the Christ event God has given the clearest, fullest, most complete, and truest expression of God's intentions for humankind, a case that even Macmurray accepts (especially in *The Clue to History*) while developing his metaphysical ontology of God's actions in the world.

Theology Without Metaphysics: Kevin Hector

Contemporary writer Kevin Hector extends Barth's mistrust of human ways of knowing (of epistemology in its philosophical form) by trying to do theology without metaphysics.[19] He observes that many postmodernist writers (as we saw

---

17. Karl Barth, "Faith as Knowledge," in *Dogmatics in Outline* (New York: Harper & Row, 1959), 23.
18. Hardy, "Karl Barth," 24. Emphasis added.
19. Kevin W. Hector, *Theology Without Metaphysics* (Cambridge: Cambridge University Press, 2011).

in the first chapter) believe that all human language is inherently metaphysical and as such "shoehorns objects into a predetermined framework and so inflicts violence upon them, and that [therefore] it must accordingly be kept at a distance from God."[20] He notes Jean-Luc Marion's claim that a God whom one could conceptualize would be no God at all. God must utterly transcend one's conception of God because conceiving God is a form of idolatry.[21] Or as John Caputo claims, language is violent because it seeks to fit objects within its horizon and to pin them down and hold them within its grip.[22] Caputo says that by naming God we wrench God into manifestation, and this puts "a violent end to God's absolute heterogeneity and holy height."[23] In short, the radical otherness of God is fatally undercut by having a metaphysical knowledge of God. But, I have argued, if metaphysics begins from the primordiality of agency and the agent, then this fear of metaphysics is profoundly misplaced.

Citing Martin Heidegger, Hector sees a parallel between Barth's rejection of natural theology and Heidegger's rejection of metaphysics. In Heidegger's view, metaphysics begins with a prior conceptual framework and determines what conceptions are acceptable and which are not. On that basis, metaphysics comes to see the being of objects as necessarily conforming to our ideas of them. As Hector states, in defense of Heidegger's view, this leads to the notion that the human person (through his conceptual apparatus) becomes to each being that upon which the manner and truth of its being is grounded. This reduces or structures the reality of the object to what conforms itself to the human conceptual framework and, in the process, obscures and negates the true reality (the radical "otherness") of the object.

It is clear that this rejection of metaphysics assumes that having a concept of God reduces God to the level of the human (as Barth clearly stated). It also assumes that to have an idea of something is to be able to control and limit that thing. But surely this is not what knowledge does if it is adequate to the reality of its object, as both Macmurray and Torrance have pointed out. If knowledge of God is adequate to God as agent, then it will "know" that God as personal agent is dynamic, living, and incapable of being wrenched, reduced, or pinned down by any ideas we have of God. Given the fact that divine agency is the supreme power of the universe and can freely supervene on the entire infrastructure of reality that God created, God always retains the upper hand and always escapes the limiting potential of human ideas.

20. Ibid., ix.
21. Ibid., 14–15.
22. Ibid., 21.
23. Ibid., 149.

Ideas represent (and then only partially) the object that they know. In that sense, the "others" (or objects) always , transcend the ideas we have of them and that is particularly true when those agent-objects have the freedom to act and to outrun our conceptions of them. Knowing God metaphysically *is* actually knowing the real God's resistance, or even inability, to be confined and restricted by human knowing and acting. Heidegger's fear of metaphysics is exorcised when it is observed that objects, especially personal dynamically acting objects, always transcend and outstrip any confining ideas we might have of them. If ideas confine reality, then no ideas would ever be appropriate to living agents since agents always push the boundaries of the ideas we have of them. The only field of knowing that might be trapped in an interpretive schema in which ideas represent static unchanging things would be science. Science might seek a conceptual knowledge of beings without the power of agency, but a theology and philosophy of agency deals with the agency of persons, and that agency always escapes, to some crucial degree, the limitations of conceptual and scientific knowledge. The primordiality of agency is the metaphysical basis on which theology can proceed without undercutting the centrality of God's acts in history.

The Necessity of Metaphysics: Wolfhart Pannenberg

A different theological voice, also in the Barthian tradition, which challenges the fear of metaphysics, and whose work is remarkably complementary to that of Macmurray and Pols, is that of German theologian Wolfhart Pannenberg. In his important book *Metaphysics and the Idea of God*, Pannenberg boldly asserted that "theological discourse about God requires a relationship to metaphysical reflection if its claim to truth is to be valid."[24] Metaphysics is the attempt to acquire a "comprehensive interpretation of the finite world."[25] Without explicitly endorsing the metaphysics of divine agency as developed along the lines of my own study, Pannenberg notes that theology is an "inquiry into God and his revelation,"[26] an inquiry that would make no sense unless it assumes the metaphysics of divine agency. Pannenberg clearly recognizes the agency of God in history in a way that is similar to that of Brueggemann and Torrance: "The God of religion is experienced primarily as a will that manifests itself in history, as the will of a holy power and hence as personal."

---

24. Wolfhart Pannenberg, *Metaphysics and the Idea of God*, trans. Philip Clayton (Grand Rapids, MI: Eerdmans, 1990), 6.
25. Ibid., 42.
26. Ibid., 12.

And he seems implicitly to accept Macmurray's notion of the confluence of theology with metaphysics when he says "when metaphysics begins to explicate the understanding of God within a particular religious tradition . . . it actually becomes theology."[27] Torrance appears to support the metaphysical claims of Pannenberg. Since "proper knowing takes place through a steady dynamic interaction between our minds and objective reality,"[28] Torrance argues that scientific theology must come to grips with the objective reality of God (and that is what metaphysics attempts to do).

Unfortunately, Pannenberg laments, the rejection of natural theology and its alliance with metaphysics "has served as an excuse for not entering seriously at all into the dialog with philosophy."[29] In fact, Pannenberg is highly critical of theologians such as Barth who overemphasize the incomprehensibility of God at the expense of God's disclosure of Godself through God's revelatory acts in history.[30] He is rightly suspicious of the view of God as a "transcendent and self-sufficient being, caught in his own transcendence and separation from the world. Rather he affirms the world . . . God is the One who is coming to establish his Kingdom in this world."[31]

He also writes in a way that echoes Macmurray's metaphysical approach when he says that "there is no metaphysics without the idea of the unity of reality."[32] The unity of the world (which in Macmurray is the unity of the world as God's act) points to a ground that is able to unify the multiplicity of the world, which for a metaphysics of agency is precisely what God's act(s) and agency do. For Pannenberg, "the whole of reality is seen as a single unity and regarded as history."[33] And "the way in which we must test any concept of God is by asking whether it can account for the unity of all reality."[34]

Of all contemporary systematic theologians, Pannenberg has the most positive assessment of history as the locus for our knowledge of God. Systematic theology, he says, "is necessary in order to substantiate the truth claims of Christian language about God. This task is met by attempting a comprehensive

27. Ibid., 41–42.

28. Thomas F. Torrance, *Christian Theology and Scientific Culture* (New York: Oxford University Press, 1981), 28.

29. Wolfhart Pannenberg, *An Introduction to Systematic Theology* (Grand Rapids, MI: Eerdmans, 1991), 25.

30. Wolfhart Pannenberg, *Faith and Reality*, trans. John Maxwell (Philadelphia: Westminster, 1977), 50–52.

31. Wolfhart Pannenberg, *Theology and the Kingdom of God* (Philadelphia: Westminster, 1969), 111.

32. Pannenberg, *Metaphysics and the Idea of God*, 22.

33. Pannenberg, *Faith and Reality*, 15.

34. Pannenberg, *Theology and the Kingdom of God*, 60.

and coherent account of the world as God's creation, including the economy of God's action in history."[35] "History is God acting in his creation. Therefore history cannot be fully understood without God. And it is not understood at all if it is conceived as the field of human action alone."[36] The biblical writings "express an increasing consciousness of God's historical activity" and the biblical understanding of reality can be compressed into a single word: "history."[37] And that history is characterized by the theme of promise and fulfillment. For Pannenberg, this means that history is not yet complete and the full revelation of God will only come at its close. "For history is a whole only when seen from the end and through that end."[38] Nevertheless, he insists—and this is his crucial theological claim—that the end has already been made present in history, proleptically, in the man Jesus Christ. This fact is the basis on which the Christian faith exists, not independent of history but precisely in history. This perfectly echoes Macmurray's claim in *The Clue to History* that Jesus fully embodied in his developed consciousness the true intention of God for history and human fulfillment.

Like Torrance, Pannenberg starts with the "fact" that God entered history when God became human in the incarnation. He also insists on the uniqueness of the resurrection of Jesus. This is the "one unique revelation of the deity of the one God."[39] But this revelation is historically situated. If, as he says, "God mediates his creation with himself through the process of history,"[40] then "Christian theology conceives the reality of God as present for our world in a specific human history," namely that of Jesus Christ.[41] And this means that "the story of Jesus Christ has to be history" at least in its core if not in all its details.[42]

Nevertheless, Pannenberg is sensitive to the fact that the conclusions of historical research are never incontestable, as we saw earlier in our reference to debates over what historians without the "eye of faith" can conclude from a reading of the biblical narrative. "If Christian faith presupposes information about events of a distant past, it can gain the greatest possible certainty about those events only by historical research."[43] This echoes Macmurray's belief that

---

35. Pannenberg, *Systematic Theology*, 13.
36. Pannenberg, *Faith and Reality*, 87.
37. Ibid., 10.
38. Ibid., 89.
39. Ibid., 60.
40. Pannenberg, *Metaphysics and the Idea of God*, 147.
41. Ibid., 139–40.
42. Pannenberg, *Systematic Theology*, 5.
43. Pannenberg, *Faith and Reality*, 71.

theology must be undogmatic and open to what the best of historiography can yield. Of course, Pannenberg, like most contemporary theologians in the Barthian tradition, accepts the resurrection of Jesus as an historical fact.

Torrance on the Importance of Space, Time, and Matter

Pannenberg, like Macmurray, makes constant reference to the "field of action" within which God and human agents interact. From the perspective developed by Pols that field of action is the infrastructure upon which agents supervene, Torrance adds to this the importance of understanding divine action in the context not only of history but also particularly of the spatio-temporal order in which divine action takes place. Torrance is particularly insistent that the core acts of God (the incarnation and the resurrection of Jesus) take place *in the world*. He decisively rejects any Kantian dualism between God and the world because it would rule out "any thought of living interaction between God and the world he has made."[44] While God is transcendent, God is not "detached from the contingent world" and the only dualism is that between the Creator and the world in which the Creator acts.[45] In this vein, Torrance implicitly evokes the notion of the causal infrastructure prominently developed by Pols. His whole understanding of God's action in the world resonates with the notion of a divine agent deploying an infrastructure (which in this case God has created) to carry out the divine intentions. The universe, Torrance says, "must be thought of as ultimately integrated from above through the creative bearing upon it of the Trinitarian relations in God himself."[46] This statement suggests the work of an Apex Being or Supreme Agent who "integrates from above" the infrastructure that God deploys to enact divine intentions just as Pols ontology of action attests. For Torrance, incarnation and resurrection "are acts of God within the contingent intelligibilities and natural structures of space and time."[47] They are in no way "an abrogation of the space-time structures of this world that we call natural laws."[48] The resurrection "was an objective act of God within the structures of space and time, within the concrete occurrences of history" and we "must interpret it as such, within the structures of space and time as we understand them."[49] When Jesus enters the world at a particular

---

44. Torrance, *Christian Theology and Scientific Culture*, 18.
45. Ibid., 56.
46. Ibid., 39.
47. Torrance, *Space, Time and Resurrection*, 22.
48. Thomas F. Torrance, *Space, Time and Incarnation* (New York: Oxford University Press, 1969), 67.
49. Torrance, *Space, Time and Resurrection*, 44.

historical moment, God "penetrates into our existence and creates room for Himself within the horizontal dimensions of finite being in space and time."[50] This penetration is perfectly consistent with the notion that God acts not by violating the natural laws but by supervening upon them or intervening into the infrastructure of space-time.

Torrance also says that incarnation and resurrection constitute the "boundary conditions" "where the natural order is open to control and explication from a higher and wider level of reality"[51] just as one would expect in an ontology of agency in which the Apex Being or Supreme Agent has at the divine disposal the whole field of action constituted by the spatio-temporal world. The highest and widest level of reality, in the ontology of action, is the being with the greatest degree of power and the greatest control over the widest possible field of action. Here, again, theology and philosophy meet because the latter develops the metaphysics of agency and the former points to the one Being, called God, who fits the description of the Supreme Agent.

Mystery Within Divine Agency

But we have left one issue still hanging: where is the mystery that the religious individual looks for in a relationship with this Supreme Agent? We have already suggested the direction in which we must go to get an adequate answer to this question. It lies at the heart of what it means to be a personal agent as such.

To get to that heart we must take one final step. Based upon what I take to be a well-justified inference that God is working out God's intentions in history, and that the major acts instantiating those intentions are to be found in the biblical narrative, I have to commit myself, in action, to a course of life in which I intend to conform to God's intentions. (If God's intentions are bound to succeed given God's power, it would be self-defeating to act in ways contrary to the divine intention.) I have to believe that my inference regarding the universal divine intention is reliable enough that it becomes a guide for my future actions. And at some indefinite point in the future I would have to experience the payoff for living according to a belief that God's intentions have been rightly inferred by me and will lead to the kind of ultimate flourishing I believe God promises those who live their lives in conformity with God's purposes. Until and unless that moment of payoff occurs, any knowledge of God from history alone must remain tentative and uncertain, requiring an act of faith, understood not as a willingness to annihilate reason, but as a

50. Ibid., 75.
51. Ibid., 22.

fundamental trust or confidence that my knowledge of God is reliable and worthy of entrusting my whole heart and mind to it.

7

Coda on the Mystery of God as Agent

Thomas Torrance has said that the field of space-time is to be referred to as "the dynamism and constancy of a living Creator." As such, it is "linked with an inexhaustible source of possibility, because of which created and historical existence is so full of endless spontaneity and surprise that there are *no rules* for the discovery of its secrets."[1] If we are truly looking for mystery in our understanding of God, how can there be anything more mysterious than an inexhaustible source of possibility, endless spontaneity, and surprise? A God beyond the reach of all human cognition, swamped in the mystical darkness of unknowing, falls into the irrelevance of intellectual abstraction when compared to a profoundly personal God who always outruns us, surprises us through acts of amazing grace, and opens up new and hitherto unexplored possibilities for new depths of relationship.

An acting God is an efficacious God, one who can get things done where and when it matters. How could an utterly "other" and totally unintelligible God have any role to play *in the world* unless the divine agent has the capacity to act? But an acting God is no longer absolutely, qualitatively, or ontologically "other" than a primordial agent. Perhaps the mute, ineffable gesture toward a totally mysterious and unintelligible God can provide psychological satisfaction for those who need God to be beyond the reach of contaminating human contact and comprehension. This kind of mysterious God, however, could have no efficacy in the world in which we live and act. The God of absolute mystery is the God of mystification, not the God of robust mystery. If God's otherness is so great that our finite reality sinks into nothingness by comparison, or if God absorbs it into an undifferentiated oneness, then the whole notion of God's efficaciousness and relationality are thereby destroyed as well. It is only in a relational world in which distinct, but not absolutely ontologically different, beings interact with and make a difference to each other that one can even think meaningfully about what God intends and does in relation to us.

1. Thomas F. Torrance, *Space, Time and Incarnation* (New York: Oxford University Press, 1969), 73.

In the world of agency, meaningfulness emerges from the relationships between persons, through which they enhance and fulfill each other. Mutuality and interpersonal love require a giving and a taking, reciprocity on the part of all the interrelated partners or participants in that mutuality.

Of course, one could argue that the psychological (or spiritual) power of believing oneself to be in some ontological relationship with sheer unqualified mystery or in having oneself confronted by that which is absolutely "other" is very strong and even compelling. Mystery always beckons us both to go beyond ourselves and to remind us of our limitations. The inherently impossible attempt to think and then articulate the unthinkable and the ineffable can be psychologically bracing and make one feel that one is in touch with something that utterly transcends the quotidian everydayness that threatens to diminish the fullness of our being if we succumb to it without reaching out for some transcendent "otherness."

Nevertheless, in the details and nuances of everyday living, the literal and figurative touch of another person, the communication and sharing of deep emotions, and the mutuality of love and compassion between persons constitute the fullness of human being. What would be missing from the fullness of life if one were able to experience a robust, inclusive, intimate, mutual, loving relationship with other persons, including the divine Person whose actions and power of being make such relationships possible? What does the evocation of a mystery that is not contained within the fullness of relationality add to that fullness? The answer to these questions is best left to the psychologist, not the philosopher of religion or the theologian. No matter how intense and stimulating the appeal of unmitigated mystery, in the end most of us want our flourishing and fulfillment to come in and through our *relationships* with other persons. And if this is true, then God, if God is to be efficacious, must meet us, embrace us, and relate to us as one person to another person.

So the challenge is to find enough mystery for the fullness of life in the relationship between persons (one of whom is God), a mystery that will satisfy our craving for the undefinable, the unsayable, the unthinkable, and the unmanipulable. We know, of course, that we cannot be fulfilled and the potentiality for full flourishing cannot be found in relationships with things that are less than personal. Inanimate objects cannot provide human persons with the necessary mutuality to constitute a fulfilling, flourishing life. Even relationships with animate objects that are less than fully human cannot do this (though some cat or dog lovers might disagree).

According to Edward Pols, the "primary being or one of its acts is the bearer of a Being that transcends it."[2] Pols admits a certain "ontological mystery" here: it is the mystery of the "concrete particular whose very particularity includes a union with and dependence upon a general, common, or universal power."³ Our power as human beings depends upon and flows from the reality of a power that encompasses us, grounds and sustains us, and brings us to fulfillment. Why this is the case, why the Apex Being has chosen to interpenetrate the world and to stand in a loving relationship with it and us, is perhaps always beyond knowing—the ultimate mystery. No list of reasons will fully explain why the woman to whom I've been married for nearly a half-century still loves me. But this is the mystery of love and love is beyond explanation. The theologians may tell us where their religious communities experience the interpenetration of the divine love and human love. But love itself is the deepest mystery of all and its expression is best left to the poet, not to the philosopher. This, I would contend, is the mystery that lies at the heart of existence. If it leads us into a dynamic, ongoing, and ever deepening relationship with the agent whose power and exercise of loving agency enables us to enjoy the full fruits of relationship, then it is mystery enough for the living of our lives.

---

2. Edward Pols, "The Ontology of the Rational Agent," *Review of Metaphysics* 33, no. 4 (June 1980): 709.

3. Edward Pols, *Meditation on a Prisoner: Towards Understanding Action and Mind* (Carbondale, IL: Southern Illinois University Press, 1975), 332.

Bibliography

Works Cited

Alston, William P. "An Action-Plan Interpretation of Purposive Explanations of Actions. In *Theory and Decision* 20, no. 3 (1986): 275–99.

———. "Divine Action: Shadow or Substance." In *The God Who Acts*, edited by Thomas F. Tracy, 41–62. University Park, PA: Pennsylvania State University Press, 1994.

———. "God's Action in the World." In *Divine Nature and Human Language: Essays in Philosophical Theology*, 197–222. Ithaca, NY: Cornell University Press, 1994.

Barth, Karl. "Faith as Knowledge." In *Dogmatics in Outline*, translated by G.T. Thompson, 22–27. New York: Harper & Row, 1959.

Bauerschmidt, Frederick Christian. "Michel de Certeau (1925–1986): Introduction." In *The Postmodern God: A Theological Reader*, edited by Graham Ward, 135–58. Malden, MA: Blackwell, 1998.

Bett, Henry. *John Scotus Erigena*. Cambridge: Cambridge University Press, 1925; New York: Russell & Russell, 1964.

Blakney, Raymond B., trans. *Meister Eckhart: A Modern Translation.* New York: Harper & Brothers, 1941.

Brueggemann, Walter. *Theology of the Old Testament*. Minneapolis: Fortress Press, 1997.

Brümmer, Vincent. "Farrer, Wiles and the Causal Joint." In *Modern Theology* 8, no. 1 (January 1992): 1–14.

Bultmann, Rudolf. *Jesus Christ and Mythology*. New York: Scribner, 1958.

Burrell, David. *Knowing the Unknowable God: Ibn-Sina, Maimonides, Aquinas.* Notre Dame, IL: University of Notre Dame Press, 1986.

Caputo, John. "God is Wholly Other—Almost: '*Différance*' and the Hyperbolic Alterity of God." In *The Otherness of God*, edited by Orrin Summerell, 190–205,. Charlottesville, VA: University Press of Virginia, 1998.

Carlson, Thomas A. "Postmetaphysical Theology." In *The Cambridge Companion to Postmodern Theology*, edited by Kevin Vanhoozer, 58–76. Cambridge: Cambridge University Press, 2003.

Carter, Robert E. *The Nothingness Beyond God: An Introduction to the Philosophy of Nishida Kitarō*. New York: Paragon House, 1989.

Clayton, Philip. *Adventures in the Spirit: God, World, Divine Action.* Edited by Zachary Simpson. Minneapolis: Fortress Press, 2008.

———. *Mind and Emergence: From Quantum to Consciousness.* Oxford: Oxford University Press, 2004.

———. *The Problem of God in Modern Thought.* Grand Rapids, MI: Eerdmans, 2000.

Colledge, Edmund, and Bernard McGinn, trans. *Meister Eckhart: The Essential Sermons, Commentaries, Treatises, and Defense.* New York: Paulist, 1981.

Coreth, Emerich. *Metaphysics.* New York: Seabury, 1973. English edition by Joseph Donceel, with a critique by Bernard Lonergan.

Derrida, Jacques. "From *How to Avoid Speaking.*" In *The Postmodern God: A Theological Reader*, edited by Graham Ward, 167–90. Malden, MA: Blackwell, 1998.

Dupré, Louis. *Religion and the Rise of Modern Culture.* Notre Dame, IN: University of Notre Dame Press, 2008.

———. "*Unio mystica:* The State and the Experience." In *Mystical Experience and Monotheistic Faith: An Ecumenical Dialogue*, edited by Moshe Idel and Bernard McGinn. New York: Macmillan, 1989.

Farrer, Austin. *Faith and Speculation.* London: Adam & Charles Black, 1967.

———. *The Freedom of the Will.* London: Adam & Charles Black, 1958.

Ford, David E., ed. *The Modern Theologians.* With Rachel Muers. Malden, MA: Blackwell, 2005.

Gibbs, Robert. "Emmanuel Levinas (1906–1995): Introduction." In *The Postmodern God: A Theological Reader*, edited by Graham Ward, 45–51. Malden, MA: Blackwell, 1998.

Gilkey, Langdon. "Cosmology, Ontology, and the Travail of Biblical Language." In *Journal of Religion* 41 (1961): 194–205.

Gilson, Etienne. *The Christian Philosophy of St. Thomas Aquinas.* New York: Random House, 1956.

Hardy, Daniel W. "Karl Barth." In *The Modern Theologians*, edited by David E. Ford with Rachel Muers, 21–42. Malden, MA: Blackwell, 2005.

Hart, Kevin. "Jacques Derrida (b. 1930): Introduction." In *The Postmodern God: A Theological Reader*, edited by Graham Ward, 159–67. Malden, MA: Blackwell, 1998.

Haught, John. *God After Darwin: A Theology of Evolution.* Boulder, CO: Westview, 2008.

Hebblethwaithe, Brian, and Edward Henderson, eds. *Divine Action: Studies Inspired by the Philosophical Theology of Austin Farrer*. Edinburgh: T&T Clark, 1990.

Hector, Kevin W. *Theology Without Metaphysics*. Cambridge: Cambridge University Press, 2011.

Hegel, G.W.F. *On Art, Religion, Philosophy: Introductory Lectures to the Realm of Absolute Spirit*. Edited by and Introduction by J. Glenn Gray. New York: Harper & Row, 1970.

Kaufman, Gordon. "On the Meaning of 'Act of God.'" In *Harvard Theological Review* 61 (1968): 175–201.

Lessing, G.E. "On the Proof of the Spirit and of Power." In *Lessing's Theological Writings*. Edited and translated by Henry Chadwick, 51–56. Stanford, CA: Stanford University Press, 1956.

Macmurray, John. *The Clue to History*. London: Student Christian Movement Press, 1938.

———. *Interpreting the Universe*. London: Faber & Faber, 1933.

———. *Persons in Relation*. Introduction by Frank G. Kirkpatrick. New York: Humanities Press, 1991.

———. *The Self as Agent*. London: Faber & Faber, 1957.

Marion, Jean-Luc. "Metaphysics and Phenomenology: A Summary for Theologians." In *The Postmodern God: A Theological Reader*, edited by Graham Ward, 279–96. Malden, MA: Blackwell, 1998.

Matthews, Eric. *The Philosophy of Merleau-Ponty*. Montreal: McGill-Queens University Press, 2002.

Moltmann, Jürgen. *God in Creation: A New Theology of Creation and the Spirit of God*. San Francisco: Harper & Row, 1985.

———. *The Trinity and the Kingdom*. San Francisco: Harper & Row, 1981.

Morreall, John. *Analogy and Talking About God: A Critique of the Thomistic Approach*. Washington, DC: University Press of America, 1979.

Munitz, Milton. *The Question of Reality*. Princeton, NJ: Princeton University Press, 1990.

Pannenberg, Wolfhart. *Faith and Reality*. Translated by John Maxwell. Philadelphia: Westminster, 1977.

———. *An Introduction to Systematic Theology*. Grand Rapids, MI: Eerdmans, 1991.

———. *Metaphysics and the Idea of God*. Translated by Philip Clayton. Grand Rapids, MI: Eerdmans, 1990.

———. *Theology and the Kingdom of God*. Philadelphia: Westminster, 1969.

Peacocke, Arthur. *Creation and the World of Science*. Oxford: Clarendon, 1979.

———. "God's Interaction with the World." In *Chaos and Complexity: Scientific Perspectives on Divine Action*. 2nd ed. Edited by Robert John Russell, Nancey Murphy, and Arthur Peacocke. Berkeley, CA: Vatican Observatory and The Center for Theology and the Natural Sciences, 1997.

———. *Theology for a Scientific Age*. Oxford: Basil Blackwell, 1990.

Plantiga, Alvin. *Warranted Christian Belief*. New York: Oxford University Press, 2000.

Pols, Edward. *The Acts of Our Being: A Reflection on Agency and Responsibility*. Amherst, MA: University of Massachusetts Press, 1982.

———. "Human Agents as Actual Beings." In *Process Studies* 8, no. 2 (Summer 1978): 103–13.

———. "Knowing God Directly." In *International Journal for Philosophy of Religion* 45:31–49 (1999): 31–49.

———. *Meditation on a Prisoner: Towards Understanding Action and Mind*. Carbondale, IL: Southern Illinois University Press, 1975.

———. *Mind Regained*. Ithaca, NY: Cornell University Press, 1998.

———. "The Ontology of the Rational Agent." In *Review of Metaphysics* 33, no. 4 (June 1980): 689–710.

———. "Power and Agency." In *International Philosophical Quarterly* 11, no. 3 (September 1971): 293–313.

Rorem, Paul, *Pseudo-Dionysius*. New York: Oxford University Press, 1993.

Russell, Robert John, Nancey Murphy, and Arthur Peacocke, eds. *Chaos and Complexity: Scientific Perspectives on Divine Action*. 2nd ed. Berkeley, CA: Vatican Observatory and The Center for Theology and the Natural Sciences, 1997.

Saunders, Nicholas. *Divine Action and Modern Science*. Cambridge: Cambridge University Press, 2002.

Stace, Walter T. *The Teachings of the Mystics*. New York: New American Library, 1960.

Summerell, Orrin, ed. *The Otherness of God*. Charlottesville, VA: University Press of Virginia, 1998.

Tallis, Raymond. *The Hand: A Philosophical Inquiry Into Human Being*. Edinburgh: Edinburgh University Press, 2003.

———. *I Am: A Philosophical Inquiry Into First-Person Being*. Edinburgh: Edinburgh University Press, 2004.

———. *The Knowing Animal: A Philosophical Inquiry Into Knowledge and Truth*. Edinburgh: Edinburgh University Press, 2005.

Taylor, Mark C. *After God*. Chicago: University of Chicago Press, 2007.

———. *Erring: A Postmodern A/Theology*. Chicago: University of Chicago Press, 1984.

Tillich, Paul. *Systematic Theology*. Vol. 1. Chicago: University of Chicago Press, 1951.

Torrance, Thomas F. *Christian Theology and Scientific Culture*. New York: Oxford University Press, 1981.

———. *God and Rationality*. New York: Oxford University Press, 1971.

———. *Space, Time and Incarnation*. New York: Oxford University Press, 1969.

———. *Space, Time and Resurrection*. Grand Rapids, MI: Eerdmans, 1976.

Tortchinov, Evgueni. "Studies in Sabbatian Kaballah: Isaac Luria's 'ZimZum.'" http://www.kheper.net/topics/Kabbalah/Tzimtzum-ET.htm.

Tracy, Thomas F. "Divine Action, Created Causes, and Human Freedom." In *The God Who Acts: Philosophical and Theological Explorations*, edited by Thomas F. Tracy, 77–102. University Park, PA: Pennsylvania State University Press, 1994.

———. "Narrative Theology and the Acts of God." In *Divine Action: Studies Inspired by the Philosophical Theology of Austin Farrer*. Edited by Brian Hebblethwaithe and Edward Henderson, 173–96. Edinburgh, T&T Clark, 1990.

Turner, Denys. *The Darkness of God: Negativity in Christian Mysticism*. Cambridge: Cambridge University Press, 1995.

Vanhoozer, Kevin, ed. *The Cambridge Companion to Postmodern Theology*. Cambridge: Cambridge University Press, 2003.

Ward, Graham, ed. *The Postmodern God: A Theological Reader*. Malden, MA: Blackwell, 1998.

Ward, Keith. *Divine Action*. London: Collins, 1990.

Wiles, Maurice. *God's Action in the World*. London: SCM, 1986.

Works Consulted

Clayton, Philip. "Tracing the Lines: Constraint and Freedom in the Movement from Quantum Physics to Theology." In *Quantum Mechanics: Scientific Perspectives on Divine Action*. Edited by Robert John Russell, Philip Clayton, Kirk Wegter-McNelly, and John Polkinghorne, 211–34. Berkeley, CA: Vatican Observatory and The Center for Theology and the Natural Sciences, 2001.

Levinas, Emmanuel. "God and Philosophy." In *The Postmodern God: A Theological Reader*, edited by Graham Ward, 52–73. Malden, MA: Blackwell, 1998.

Peacocke, Arthur. "God's Action in the Real World." In *Zygon* 26, no. 4 (December 1991): 455–76.

Index

Act of Being, 20, 29, 58, 120, 121
agency, vii, xiii–xiv, 1–5, 9, 15–17, 19, 21, 23, 36–37, 43–44, 49, 52, 60–62, 65–69, 71–87, 90, 92–93, 87–107, 113–14, 122, 125–27, 129–32, 144–46, 149, 152
Alston, William, 120–23
anthropomorphism, vii, xii, 3, 6–8, 17, 23, 26, 49–50, 63, 65, 68, 103–6
apex being, xi, 91, 96–97, 100, 103, 124, 126, 148–49, 153
apophatic, xiv, 26–27, 31, 52–53, 63
Aquinas, Thomas, 27, 32, 51, 104–5
Aufhebung, 36, 47–48

Barth, Karl, 24, 29, 39, 129, 133, 142–46
basho, 44–45
basic actions, 121
Being-Itself, 4, 10, 38–39, 44
Brueggemann, Walter, 133–34, 145
Brummer, Vincent, 114
Bultmann, Rudolf, 111–14
Burrell, David, 30

Caputo, John, 38, 144
Carlson, Thomas A, 41
causality, xiv, 11–12, 19, 78, 80, 84–89, 96, 101, 111, 113, 115, 118–19, 124, 128
Clayton, Philip, xii, x–xi, 11, 124–26
Colledge, Edmund, 52
continuant, 75, 83–86, 89
Coreth, Emerich, 32–37, 40, 45
creation, vii, 12, 15, 18–19, 27, 29, 37, 40, 42, 53, 55, 73, 117, 123, 125, 132, 142, 147
creationism, viii–x

Dawkins, Richard, viii, 65
de Certeau, Michel, 43
Derrida, Jacques, 42
Descartes, Rene, 62, 71
detachment, 57
différance, 38, 42
differentiation, 27–32, 35–36, 45, 48, 51, 55, 59, 71, 75–76, 100, 107
disinterest, 57
dualism, xii, 3, 7–9, 16, 23, 28–30, 32, 44–45, 48–49, 51, 53, 59–60, 70, 73, 90, 103, 107, 112, 125–28, 148
Dupre, Louis, 50

Eckhart, Meister, 34, 46, 48, 50–58, 71, 100, 126
Erigena, John Scotus, 31–32, 45
evil, 17–18
evolution, viii–ix, xi, 14, 17, 64–65, 75–76, 132
existential intuition (EI), 71
explanatory ultimacy, 91–92, 95

Farrer, Austin, 113–14
freedom, xv, 3, 6, 11, 13, 18, 47, 69–70, 77, 93, 106, 112, 132–33, 142, 145

Gilkey, Langdon, 111–12, 140
God as Agent, vii–viii, xiii, 6, 10, 17–18, 37, 82, 90, 97, 106–7, 116, 130–31, 135, 151
Godhead, 38, 51, 53–55

Haught, John, ix–xi, 125
Hector, Kevin, 129, 143–44
Hegel, G.W.F., 36, 47–48
Heidegger, Martin, 144–45

history, vii, xiii, 17–18, 73, 111–14, 129–31, 133–43, 145–49

infrastructure, x–xii, xv, 11, 18–20, 65–70, 77, 83–88, 91–96, 100–101, 109–10, 114, 118, 121, 124, 130, 136, 144, 148–49
intelligent design, viii–xi, 14, 17
intentions/intentionality, x–xi, xv, 4–7, 11, 16, 18–20, 49, 64–65, 67, 70, 74, 76–78, 80–86, 88–89, 91, 95–96, 106, 110, 116, 119, 121, 123–24, 131–39, 141–43, 147–49
interference, viii, xiv, 19–20, 84, 110, 119–20, 123–24
intervention, x, xiv, 12, 19, 78, 87–88, 95, 110, 116–20, 123–28, 140

Jesus, 15, 111, 132–33, 139, 141–42, 147–48
John XXII, Pope, 52

Kant, Immanuel, xv, 60, 112, 148
Kaufman, Gordon, 111–12, 114, 140
Kitaro, Nishida, 44

Lessing, G.E., 131, 140
Levinas, Emmanuel, 42
Luria, Isaac, 37

Macmurray, John, xiv, 62–69, 72–77, 79, 81–86, 88–92, 96, 102–7, 119–23, 126–27, 131–35, 137, 143–48
Marion, Jean-Luc, 41–43
Matthews, Eric, 72
McGinn, Bernard, 50, 52
Merleau-Ponty, Maurice, 72
metaphysics, ix, 2, 31–33, 41, 43–46, 54, 104, 124, 129–30, 134, 143–49
Michelangelo, 73
Moltmann, Jurgen, 37

monism, xii, 7–9, 23–24, 27–34, 44, 48–51, 57–60, 70, 73, 90, 103, 106, 126–28
mystery, vii–viii, xii–xvi, 1–7, 11, 18, 30–36, 39, 46, 49, 54, 63, 66, 69, 93, 99–100, 103, 111, 127, 149, 151–53
mysticism, xii, 34, 37, 48–50, 54, 58–59, 100

nothingness, 31, 44–46, 63, 151

oneness, xiv, 9–10, 20, 23, 26, 34, 36, 45, 48–51, 54, 57–59, 63, 71, 90, 100, 103, 107, 126–28, 151
ontic power, 86, 90
ontological transcendence, 3, 20, 26, 30, 58, 90, 106–7
Otherness, 4, 8–10, 16, 23–26, 28–32, 34, 36–38, 40–41, 43–44, 47–51, 57–58, 63, 90, 103, 106–8, 126, 144, 151–52

panentheism, 37, 125–28
Pannenberg, Wolfhart, 2, 130, 136, 145–48
Peacocke, Arthur, x–xi, xiv, 11, 124–26
Plantinga, Alvin, 136–37
Pols, Edward, xi, xiv, 11, 65–67, 77–81, 84–106, 109–10, 112, 116, 118–27, 134, 140, 145, 148, 152–53
prayer, 1, 12, 14, 18, 20–21, 80
primary being, 91, 98–103, 127, 152
primordiality, x–xi, xiii, 2–3, 5, 9, 15, 18, 21, 51, 53–54, 57, 61–65, 78–79, 85, 93, 96, 99, 102, 118, 127–31, 134–35, 144–45
process thought, 132
Pseudo-Dionysius, 26–27, 52–53

quantum level, 115–18, 122

reductionism, xii, xii, 86, 93, 119–20
Reid, Thomas, 75

relationality, xiv, 2, 4, 8, 34, 39, 51, 55, 57, 66, 73–74, 105, 151–52
religious experience, viii, 11, 45–46, 52, 138, 141
resistance, 48, 66, 73–75, 82–83, 105–6, 145
Rorem, Paul, 27
Russell, Robert, 115–16, 125

Saunders, Nicholas, 115, 117
Scripture, vii, xiii, 12, 14–5, 17, 19–20, 139–40
Stace, W.T., 34, 51, 58–59
STMW (Spatio-Temporal-Material-World), 6–7, 12–13, 15, 19, 24–25, 30–31, 59, 63, 65, 71, 79–80
supervention, 94–96, 124, 127, 140

Tallis, Raymond, xiv, 65–79, 84, 90, 104–7, 118–19, 123, 134
Taylor, Mark C., 9, 40, 45
Tillich, Paul, 38–39, 53
Torrance, Thomas, 133–34, 138, 144–49, 151
Tracy, Thomas, 113–14, 117–18, 122
Turner, Denys, 27, 29

U-factor, 98–99, 101, 127
Ward, Keith, 113
Whitehead, Alfred North, xi, 97, 125
wholly other, 4, 13, 24, 38–39, 143
Wiles, Maurice, 114

ZimZum, 37

www.ingramcontent.com/pod-product-compliance
Lightning Source LLC
Chambersburg PA
CBHW071204070526
44584CB00019B/2905